MW00804367

YOUR OWN ITALY TRAVEL GUIDE

THE FAST TRACK FOR DIVERSE TRAVELERS TO PLANNING SAFE ADVENTURES, DISCOVERING HIDDEN GEMS, LEARNING LOCAL LINGO, AND EXPERIENCING AUTHENTIC ITALIAN CULTURE

MARIA TUMINELLI

YOUR BEST
PUBLISHING
LLC

CONTENTS

INTRODUCTION

 If you don't try, nothing ever changes.

ELENA FERRANTE, *MY BRILLIANT FRIEND* (2018)

Roma! The very name takes a trip: a slight trill of the *R*, gently rounding into an *Oh*, all to land one final punch on *Ma*! *Rr-oh-ma.* There's no way you can say it without experiencing some form of excitement.

Perhaps I'd been reading too much Elena Ferrante. I'd been trying to get my head around one of Europe's most fascinating cultures, but as I made my way through Rome's Termini station, I felt a pang of excitement. Despite my luggage, I didn't feel much like a tourist–I'd read enough guides on Italy to know just what to do.

Or so I thought.

Sailing through the busy barriers to the open gate for passengers with large luggage, I found my platform and boarded accordingly. This was the beginning of the two weeks I'd planned to travel solo around the peninsula, with one week spent in the capital and the next in Naples— the famous "City of Pizza." Freshly single, I was all too ready to get back out there and seize the day (*carpe diem*). This trip, I'd hoped, would be my ultimate *Eat, Pray, Love* moment (Murphy, 2010).

So, there I was, in the second car of a stuffy subway heading southwest toward my modest two-star hotel. "Perfect for solo travelers," my favorite hotel booking website had said.

"Excuse me, miss."

The Italian accent, thick like a perfect Alfredo sauce, hit me hard.

"Your ticket, please?"

The ticket inspector was dressed in ordinary clothes. The cuff of his washed-out red shirt stretched before me, expecting me to press my papers into his palm.

Which I didn't have.

As I rushed through the events leading up to this awkward situation, my mind immediately recalled the moment at the barrier gates. It had been so packed that I'd managed to get swept up by the tides of tourists, seamlessly passing the open gates only to end up here, on this train, with no valid ticket.

I wasn't sure if I should even pretend to look for what I already knew wasn't there. I sat paralyzed when a woman who'd been standing behind the man slowly turned to face me–another inspector.

Julia Roberts would never be caught dead in this mess (Murphy, 2010).

Ten minutes later and 50€ lighter, I sulked out from the train at Colosseo station. My two weeks of sun and self-discovery had not gotten off to a great start. In hindsight, the trip did turn out to be a lot of fun by the end, but I often cringe when I think back on how it all began. I regret that my first real-life encounter with this vibrant city–let alone Italy as a country–almost ten years ago was met with a fine I couldn't really afford.

Since that dreadful morning, I have experienced hurdle after hurdle of challenges while exploring this boot-shaped peninsula. From hitching overnight trains along the north's craggy Alps to having to pay twice as much when the bill arrived after a misunderstanding due to my early lack of skill in Italian, my ten years exploring this jewel of the Mediterranean as a tourist-turned-student-turned-expat continue to pique my curiosity to this very day.

Although *I* might have lost out on ordering an extra twenty gelatos during my first trip in Rome (worth exactly 50€), this guide is an attempt to make sure *you* definitely won't!

Beyond any anxieties you might have about making mistakes similar to the ones I just mentioned, you might also feel like the sheer number of travel options in Italy has been curbing your wanderlust. Maybe scrolling through social media only to hear two contradicting views on the exact same activity seems to suck all the spontaneity out of planning your getaway to the Amalfi Coast or the canals of Venice.

And rightly so. It can be maddening to create an itinerary you have confidence in. Plus, the context in which you will be traveling could make the process seem even harder. As a seasoned solo traveler who's also openly Queer, I can hand-on-heart admit to having had my own fair share of mishaps abroad. I've been there, whether it was getting my things stolen at a restaurant when using the restroom, missing my ferry because I wasn't running fast enough, or even having to avoid uncalled-for looks and comments.

Traveling alone, no matter your identity, can bring up a lot of awkwardness, which I'd like to debunk throughout the pages of this humble guide. While I hope my writing will reach out to everyone ready to dive into Italian culture, those who identify as Queer or anywhere else on the LGBTQIA+ wheel of color, in particular, can read along feeling confident that some of the tensions they may have felt have been carefully considered. No one, no matter their age, race, or sexual orientation, should ever have to compromise, especially during recreational travel. Fear not—this guide will provide all the inclusive insights you need!

Likewise, traveling "in bulk" can sometimes make you forget that you're on vacation in the first place; there are so many factors to consider. So, if you're planning to visit Italy with friends, family, or your partner and secretly dreading all the stressful strings attached, this book is also for you. You'll never have to worry about how to satisfy everyone's Italian sightseeing requests again!

So, kick back and take a deep breath! This tried and tested guide will give you curated recommendations to help you save valuable time on research so that you can plunge back into the joy of planning your perfect trip. As you read, you'll encounter first-hand experiences from me and some anecdotes I've collected not only from friends and family but also from strangers during my adventures. My aim is to lay bare these travel experiences by letting them write themselves. Through learning from this collective of fellow travelers, you'll be able to avoid common mistakes and make your own timeless memories while you explore!

Not only this, but you will be able to brush up on your Italian, as we will cover the essential phrases for getting around the country. While food may be the fastest way to one's heart, speaking the language has the same ability to pull at the locals' heartstrings. Using even a few simple words can make a lasting impression, allowing your travel experience to flow as easily as the unique connections you'll make with the nation's wonderfully unforgettable people.

Since we will be covering a lot of information here, remember that this book isn't meant to be read from cover to cover. Instead, I have divided the text into chapters covering topics and scenarios that best suit your needs, so feel free to skip to the ones that apply directly to you.

So, without further ado, let's embark on our journey to one of Europe's most important cultural crossroads: *Italy*.

CHAPTER 1
DISCOVERING YOUR ITALIAN ADVENTURE

 Nel blu, dipinto di blu (In the blue [sky], I'm painted blue*)*

NEL BLU DIPINTO DI BLU (1958)

BEAUTIFUL COUNTRY (*BEL PAESE*)

Chances are that if you've picked up this book, you're considering a trip to the Beautiful Country (*Bel Paese*) of Italy. Here are some of its unique aspects that tempt travelers from all over the world …

It is impossible to venture through the Italian peninsula without experiencing the country's sense of vibrant theatrics. Scanning the nation from top to bottom, one can clearly feel that the world is indeed a stage. All one has to do is consider the meticulously manicured parks and gardens almost as set designs. Even the natural backgrounds blend into the drama of the country, with its statuesque cypresses, sprawling fig trees, and chorus rows of vineyards. Such scenes have been the chosen backdrops of paintings by da Vinci, Bellini, and Titian throughout history (*see Chapter 5 for more information on Italy's artistic heritage*).

The show continues to unfold as one wanders through Italian cities. Take Venice, for example. One magical moment inspires you to meander through its winding lanes, with the towering five-story apartments nearby pushing you into the spotlight of a dazzling public square (*piazza*) like the one named after Saint Mark (San Marco). As you travel, you will quickly learn the importance of *piazze* (that's the plural) as spaces that fulfill the need of Mediterranean people to freely conduct their lives in the open air.

No theater is ever really complete without blissful music, another art medium that descends from a long cultural heritage rooted in Italy. Opera was born in Florence more than 400 years ago during the Renaissance, and its virtuosic traces can still be appreciated on the very pavements of many towns and cities today. As the sun rolls into the late afternoon, clusters of street musicians take the cooler temperatures as an opportunity to burst into song, accompanied by a violin or perhaps an accordion.

You may also see signs of the sweet life (*la dolce vita*) through the animated gestures of the locals as they argue their way through business, politics, or football (soccer)–more often football than politics. These showdowns can occur suddenly and at any time in any location, though this performance is usually preferred seated at a favorite café over an espresso. No people more joyfully live up to their legendary image than the Italians (*see Chapter 4 for how to use local lingo*).

At even the simplest informal restaurant (*trattoria*), one is guaranteed a presentation to heighten the senses. Even before you find your table, your meal has begun. Not with the menu, mind you, but with a display of platters of purple squid and pink scampi, glistening ribbons of pappardelle pasta, juicy zucchini, stuffed eggplant, and bowls dripping with fresh grapes. If your journey allows, you may even get the chance to see the fruit harvest and, better yet, taste the succulent wines that are a staple of the Italian diet (*see Chapter 5 for tasty food recommendations*).

The table of delights extends from the conventionally more prosperous, industrial north down to the warmer south. A trip down the length of the peninsula and to the islands will reveal all the richness and variety that the Bel Paese has to offer: from the purple-headed Dolomites and the snow-capped Alps to the glittering waters of Lake Como, the lagoons of Venice, the shallow foundations of Pisa's celebrated Tower, and of course, the distinguished port city of Palermo in Sicily. There's truly something for everyone here, from the hustle and bustle of the larger cities to the hidden gems to be found among its many towns and villages (*see more on these in Chapter 3*). Boasting 59 UNESCO World Heritage Sites, Italy is also home to some of the most significant archaeological structures in the world (*see Chapters 3 and 5 for more information).* It seems every corner is packed with history. The "Eternal City" of Rome has witnessed countless declines and rebirths and still valiantly resists all of modernity's threatening assaults. The ruins of Pompeii offer time capsules from another world, all at once so foreign and yet so accessible.

The Italian people, with Latins and Etruscans mixing over the centuries with Greeks, Lombards, Normans, and Spaniards, are as diverse as the country's mélange of landscapes. Given its relatively brief history as a unified nation since 1861, Italians' patriotic sense is (arguably) invested in the national football (soccer) team. While most of them are naturally cheerful and friendly toward foreigners, it must be noted that much scorn is reserved domestically–namely, between the north and south divide. Beyond the array of regional identifications, the country stands culturally divided, and has remained so over centuries of imposing feudal rule in Naples and Sicily while the north boosted economic development.

Yet, this complex background merely nuances the warm-hearted, high-spiritedness of the general population, much of which can be experienced during major carnivals and festivals like Venice's masquerading Festival (Festa Veneziana) *(see Chapter 5 for more on this and many other local celebrations).*

Many mistake the Italian sense of style perhaps for snobbishness, but look closely and you will see it is not always so much about "dressing up" as about dressing *well.* Modern Italian fashion is comfortable in its own fabric, sporting national quirks such as the unisex leather moccasins, imperatively worn *without* socks. The high streets of Milan and Rome will surely cater to your every clothing whim.

In the sincerest of summaries, Italy is a spectacle on which the curtains are never drawn. These are merely a few of the reasons why anyone should visit this magical place!

WHEN TO TRAVEL TO ITALY?

This is not an easy decision. The vastly diverse climates, landscapes, and festivities might seem overwhelming. But it's helpful to bear in mind that not even the most nomadic of visitors has completely "done" the entire country; that's the charm of travel. If the seduction works—and it will—you will find yourself on countless return flights in the future. During the initial stages, it's always better to plan your destination(s) around your availability, budget, and travel style–a few of which we will dive into. Don't let the fear of missing out creep up on you; no matter the time of year you plan on traveling there, the Italian nation and its people will welcome you with open arms.

Seasons

Weatherwise, the most pleasant months to travel to Italy are May, June, September, and October. These months offer comfortable daytime temperature averages of 77°F (25°C) and 59°F (15°C) at night. Of course, these temperatures vary from region to region, so be prepared for cooler temperatures in northern areas like Milan and Venice compared to the more central areas like Naples. The only downside to these months is that May is considered the peak season for tourism, so it will be more crowded then.

If those dates aren't possible, consider heading north during the sweltering months of July and August, when temperatures in cities farther south like Rome, Florence, and Naples can rise well above 95°F (35°C).

Many perceptions of beautiful Italy (*Bella Italia*) immediately evoke the heat; the idea of traveling during the wintertime is not so common. This is a secret we might like to keep. If you don't mind bundling up for 41°F (13°C), try to go during the transition period from fall to winter between November and February. I guarantee that lines to the Vatican or Basilica San Marco (St. Mark's Basilica) will be a lot shorter. You might even be able to grab a gondola down the Grand Canal in Venice and still have time left over for another circuit!

Public Holidays

And remember, Italians make no bones about closing on public holidays. One time, while passing through Spoleto on an excursion, I had a window of five hours between train layovers. I thought I could quickly visit the city's main cathedral to see the Lippi frescoes, which would be a great way to pass the time.

Wrong! The doors were bolted. It was November 1.

I'd neglected to search ahead of time for that particular date and was left stranded on the church's steps, munching my focaccia sandwich for breakfast at eight in the morning. So, please don't be like me and make that same unfortunate mistake.

For better or worse, on public holidays in Italy, it can often feel like the whole country is either in hibernation or a total party frenzy, which, depending on your preferences, could still be a good time!

Italy has ten national holidays (*feste*) each year. When one falls on a Thursday or a Tuesday, Italians may make a bridge (*ponte*) to the weekend so that Friday and Monday are also written off. While some other cultures "live to work," Italians clearly "work to live"–and rightfully so!

Here's a table of all ten:

January 1	Primo dell'Anno	New Year's Day
January 6	Epifania	Epiphany
Moveable date	Lunedì di Pasqua (Pasquetta)	Easter Monday
April 25	Festa della Liberazione	Liberation Day
May 1	Festa del Lavoro	Labor Day (May Day)
August 15	Ferragosto	Assumption Day
November 1	Ognissanti	All Saints' Day
December 8	L'Immacolata Concezione	Immaculate Conception
December 25	Natale	Christmas Day
December 26	Santo Stefano	St. Stephen's Day

Setting Your Financial Course

Depending on your budget, needs, and style of travel, these tips should really be considered as a means to map out expenses rather than an end in and of themselves. For example, you might be traveling solo (which is often the most expensive option), but maybe you're okay with roughing it for a couple of nights, which could significantly lower your costs. Either way, this section has you covered.

*All amounts in this section are in euros and are subject to change. Please always research current prices and use your favorite online currency converter for accurate live rates.

*All information from *Champion Traveler* (n.d.).

Basic Budget

Solo Travelers

Traveling alone can be an enriching experience. It allows you to explore new places at your own pace and gives you the chance to fully immerse yourself in different cultures. If you're someone who enjoys independence and freedom, solo travel could be an excellent option for you.

For a one-week solo Italian trip, the cost can range from 708€ to 1,611€, which breaks down to about 101€ to 230€ per day. Here's a breakdown of the usual expenses:

- Accommodation: Roughly 39€ to 47€ per night for a basic 1-star hotel room or 50€ to 78€ per night for a one-bedroom vacation rental.
- Flights: Budget between 347€ and 901€ for an economy class ticket.
- Daily Expenses: Plan for around 18€ to 34€ per day for meals, transportation, and sightseeing needs.

Couples

For a week in Italy for two people, you can expect to spend between 1,175€ to 2,747€, which is about 168€ to 392€ per day. Here's the breakdown:

- Accommodation costs range from 40€ to 46€ per night for a basic hotel room or 50€ to 78€ per night for a one-bedroom vacation rental.
- Flight prices vary between 694€ to 1,801€ for economy class.
- Budget around 34€ to 69€ per day for meals, transportation, and sightseeing for both of you.

Families (Of Four)

For a week-long family trip for four people, the cost starts at around 2,312€ to 5,266€ (330€ to 752€ per day):

- Stay: 80€ to 93€ per night for two 1-star hotel rooms or 74€ to 116€ per night for a 2-bedroom vacation rental
- Flights: 1,388€ to 3,601€ on economy class
- Meals, travel, and activities: 69€ to 138€ per day for all four people's daily expenses

Tips for Budget Travelers

(Champion Traveler, n.d.)

Check the Location of Your Accommodation

Depending on your choice of lodging (which we will explore in depth just after this budget section), try to select a location a little further away from the major tourist sites so you can avoid the hustle and bustle. However, that is not to say that you should neglect the historic downtown areas altogether. It is possible to remain central without staying at the doorstep of, say, the Pantheon. Busy locations like these will not only be overpriced but might also be quite uncomfortable to reach and even sleep above.

Take Advantage of *Aperitivo*

Translated to mean "to open," the traditional *aperitivo* ritual of a drink and light snack begins after the afternoon break (*riposo*) and goes from around 4 p.m.–8 p.m. to get the ball rolling again well into the night. It can be difficult to resist sitting down to a drink after a busy day of sightseeing, so if you're worried about spending too much on alcohol and snacks (and let's face it, on vacation, most of us do), then aperitivo is your saving grace–with a plate of free food served alongside every beverage ordered. Before "happy hour," there was always aperitivo!

Make Lunch the New Dinner

If your visit to the Bel Paese doesn't entail at least one succulent feast, then what's the point of life, right? However, when traveling on a budget, making lunch your main meal is a great way to save money. Lunch specials and deals are commonplace in major cities, so consider opting for those. And if you don't mind scrounging a lot, pair a big meal at lunch with a platter or two of aperitivo snacks, and you're done for the day!

Beware of a Cover Charge (*Coperto*)

No, he isn't some green-eyed monster, although *coperto* can leave your wallet dazed if you aren't paying close attention. Most bars and restaurants operate on this per-head cover charge of around 1€–3€ added to your total bill. If you're looking to grab a snack or a coffee on a budget, consider standing at the bar so you don't have to pay the cover. Likewise, meals at restaurants can often begin with chargeable servings of bread, oil, vinegar, olives, and even salt and pepper! If you're unsure whether these products cost extra, just ask. While these additions might not seem like a lot, having five or six coffees a day between yourselves for a week can amount to around 126€, which could get you an extra night somewhere or a fun day out instead.

Avoid Eating Out Near Tourist Sites

"When in Rome, do as the Romans do," and the same can be said for Italy more generally. If your accommodation has a kitchen, shopping like a local for groceries and eating in most nights will be a big money-saver. But if the opportunity to eat out does present itself, try avoiding touristy sites and leave the views for bench picnics. For food, move two or three blocks away from those busy spots and tune your ears to the surrounding spoken language. As soon as you hear more Italian being spoken inside, you've hit the jackpot. Chances are the food will be better there anyway.

Buy From Small Kiosks

Trust me when I say it—make a U-turn from kiosk vans selling drinks and snacks at busy locations! As mentioned earlier, the key to saving is going to the local supermarkets for groceries instead. Stock up in the morning before your day out so you'll be prepared!

Order a *Vino Casa*

Italy, dubbed the "Land of Wine" by the ancient Greeks, boasts a fertility like no other. The Bel Paese produces more native grapes than France, Greece, and Spain combined, so naturally, you may wish to have at least one glass of its renowned elixir. Although it may seem challenging to choose when scanning menus of options—all with various prices—simply ordering a house wine (*vino casa*) will generally get you a decent glass for a reasonable price.

Book Train Tickets in Advance

Book early and book ahead. As soon as you know where you'd like to travel, buy your tickets–don't wait until the last minute!

Choose Cities That Are More Affordable

As you can imagine, the most popular cities, like Venice, will be the most expensive. So, plan your stay by considering other destinations like Padua or Vicenza, which are not as popular and won't break your bank. Besides, you can shuttle to those popular cities for the day and return to a quieter, cheaper, more relaxed environment by sundown.

Use Public Transportation

Most of the more popular areas will provide at least one of the following public transport options: bus, subway, or tram. Naples has four funicular routes, too! These will be more affordable than hiring a driver, catching a taxi, or even ordering an Uber (available only in major cities like Milan and Rome). As with the national trains, be wary of occasional delays.

Know Free or Discounted Museum Days

Some museums and galleries are free or discounted one day each month. For example, the ruins of Pompeii are free to visit on the first Sunday. Check these in advance.

Buy City Passes

City passes like the Roma (Rome) Card and Firenze (Florence) Card can offer helpful perks like free public transportation, free or discounted access to popular historical sites, and even restaurant guides. The Firenze Card even includes other destinations in Tuscany! Check the museums included on the card(s) first to ensure they are the ones you wish to visit.

Choose Your Sites Wisely

Sightsee responsibly. "Doing" Italy is a lifetime vocation that even the most devoted travel buffs never truly "get done" with. Thank goodness for that, for to "be done" with the Bel Paese is to be done with the joys of life itself! So, be intentional with what you want to see while you're there, and savor the delights readily at hand. Consuming too much art history may leave you with a case of indigestion that has you mistaking a fire extinguisher sign for the frescos of Michelangelo!

UNDERSTANDING ACCOMMODATION OPTIONS

Hotel (Albergo)

An *albergo is* generally what the name says on the label, making it the safest accommodation choice for any type of traveler. However, while the quality of Italian hotels is graded based on a star system, these won't necessarily correspond to the star ratings you might be familiar with elsewhere. Just like anywhere else, the amenities a hotel provides can vary considerably. Some may have swimming pools, gyms, and an in-house bar and include breakfast, while others may not even have an elevator. Before you book, be sure to review the hotel description closely and contact them to confirm amenities if you're unsure about anything.

Side note: Remember that the service change, tourist tax, and VAT (sales tax) are often not included in room rates, so if prices are not listed as all-inclusive (*tutto compreso*), as much as 20% may be added to your bill.

Bed and Breakfasts

Many travelers (solo, couples, or families) use this staple accommodation style, which means roughly the same thing worldwide. Just don't expect too much on the breakfast front in Italy. Instead, try to resign yourself to a refrigerator stocked with fruit and yogurt along with a pantry of a few bags of dainty breakfast biscuits and certainly the makings for coffee. And there it is (*E ecco fatto!*)—breakfast is served! You may also book a B&B and then find it's really just a budget hotel that provides a simple breakfast buffet.

Farm Stay (Agriturismo)

No, this option does not mean what it says at a glance. I promise—there are no cow-milking expectations here. Instead, think of *agritur-*

ismo as a B&B in a farmhouse on what is often a working farm. These experiences are becoming increasingly popular since they revolve more around experiencing the rural Italian lifestyle over the average tourist city indulgences. Some stays can include outdoor activities or cooking classes, but these will vary with what the farm has available. Most of the time, your stay includes at least one meal per day, and sometimes more. These places are typically not in cities, so getting there without a car can be tricky (or impossible). As you search for accommodations, you may also see some cheaper or more basic *agriturismi* (the plural of agriturismo) listed alongside hostels.

Hostel (Ostello)

The hostels of the past featured strictly dorm-style bunks and were available only to young people. To get into an Italian youth hostel, you needed a membership card issued by the International Youth Hostel Federation or AIG (Associazione Italiana Alberghi per la Gioventù). Most hostels around the world (including in the Bel Paese) have now removed the age restrictions, providing not only smaller shared rooms but also private rooms with ensuite bath options.

True, private rooms in hostels cost more than a bed in a 10-person dorm, but they usually cost quite a bit less than a hotel room. Shared or private rooms in hostels may suit a younger couple, a group of friends, or an individual flying solo. However, I wouldn't recommend them to families, as some hostels may not accommodate children.

Also, keep in mind that in Italian, the terminology isn't always black and white; in fact, it usually operates in a gray area. It's common to see hostels advertised under the label "hotel" or "guesthouse." But, since numbers never lie, always follow the money. Especially low prices mean you're probably looking at a hostel or low-end hotel.

Vacation Rental

Families and couples staying in one place for more than a few days will find renting a furnished villa or apartment more economical, especially in resorts. In Italy, you'll find these advertised as vacation rentals, apartment rentals, and, sometimes, villa rentals.

Convents/Monasteries

Convents and monasteries have a rich history of providing accommodation for travelers through the ages, a tradition that endures today. While not all of these sacred sites cater to tourists, those that do offer budget-friendly lodging starting at just 28€ per night. Families may find restrictions, as children are often not permitted unless it explicitly states they are.

These lodgings are ideal for solo adventurers who value simplicity and don't plan on staying out late, as most establishments have curfews and lock their doors at night regardless of guests' whereabouts. Many places welcome individuals of all beliefs, while some have no religious requirements at all. Nevertheless, before making a reservation, it's essential to review the specific guidelines. Travelers, especially those journeying alone, should consider convents and monasteries to be reliable and secure accommodation options.

A key consideration for couples: These lodgings are often segregated by gender, so unmarried heterosexual pairs may encounter discomfort and are advised to seek alternative options. Moreover, for religious reasons, certain accommodations may not admit unmarried couples. Unfortunately, despite the Pope's recent strides in LGBTQIA+ inclusivity, openly Queer individuals or Queer couples might face difficulties entering these institutions due to enduring prejudices. I always recommend that you and your partner prioritize safety while traveling abroad.

HOW TO GET THERE

(The Italian on Tour, 2023).

Booking Your Flight

So now you're ready to book your plane ticket(s)! Here are some tips to help you find the perfect flight:

Start Early, Stay Flexible

It's always best to start searching as soon as you know your travel time frame. Try to stay flexible with flight dates, especially if you're on a budget, and then tailor your dates to match the fares that are closest to your price range. Since they will usually rise as you get closer to the time of your trip, you can often save a lot of money by booking your flights several months in advance.

Utilize Fare Comparison Tools

Google Flights, Skyscanner, and Kayak offer fare comparison tools that allow you to search multiple airlines and travel agencies simultaneously. You can also adjust the search options to compare prices, airlines, and the lengths of flights and layovers. You can even receive notifications when the prices for your desired flight(s) drop.

Book Directly with Airlines

After you've found an itinerary that meets your criteria, consider booking directly through the airline's official website. This cuts out the "middle man" and makes the process less stressful. Besides, many airlines can provide better customer service and more options for managing changes.

Consider Getting Assistance

If you have AAA, a credit card like American Express, or a trusted travel agent, consider utilizing their services to help you search for flights. Also, checking in with them for their latest advice on navigating fares is always a good idea.

Loyalty Programs and Miles/Kilometers

If you're a frequent traveler, maybe you're part of a points program. It's worth researching whether you can join a frequent flyer program or if your existing loyalty membership allows you to spend some points on discounts, flight upgrades, or even free airfare!

Think About Layovers

Long layovers can be an excellent opportunity to explore an additional city along the way, but they also add to your travel time. So, to find the best flights for your situation, remember to factor in the airports you'll go through and how long it'll be before you board your next plane. Some airlines even offer free layover tours! Still, I always recommend booking direct flights if those costs remain within your budget. This is because it will save you time and make any loss of luggage *a lot* less likely!

Compare Total Costs

Avoid falling into the rabbit hole of "cheap flights." While the initial amount displayed may seem dirt-cheap, this might not be the most cost-effective option after factoring in baggage fees, seat selection, and other add-ons. Always compare the total costs of your flights before making your decision.

Schedule a Midweek Departure

When possible, schedule flights for Tuesdays, Wednesdays, or Thursdays. Flying out any other day can be more expensive. Try going for a Tuesday departure (the cheapest day to travel) at a low-peak hour like 11 a.m., and then you've got your flights to Italy sorted out.

Schedule Seating

This tip is pretty subjective. Selecting specific seats can significantly increase your total cost if you're unlucky. Personally, I often sacrifice comfortable travel options to save a bit for the actual trip, but then again, I know many friends who would *never* rough it on a long voyage. So, if you think you'll need a lot of legroom, the first thing you'll want to check is the pitch, or distance between rows of seats, on the aircraft you'll be flying on. This will help you estimate how much legroom you'll have. The pitch on most modern jets is from 29–32 inches. To ensure your comfort, also plan around any other limits on space or the number of available seats. One way to secure more legroom for your flight at (perhaps) no or low additional cost is to reserve a seat in an emergency exit row, as these seats always offer more space.

Consider Flying from Nearby Airports

The best thing about flying flexibility is that you don't need to limit your search to just one airport. Considering departure and arrival airports other than those closest to you may be more economical and (in the case of Italian airports at least) may be a great way to see additional areas of the country you might not have thought to visit.

Check Travel Restrictions

Be sure to verify the current rules and regulations that may affect your travel to Italy–these change all the time. It's best to head to the official Italian government website to be sure that the country is generally safe to travel to (i.e., quarantine measures, strikes, and terrorist alerts).

CONSIDERING TRAVEL INSURANCE

Even the most seasoned travelers sometimes run into sticky situations when abroad. So, no matter how you travel, my advice is to at least consider purchasing travel insurance. Of course, this will largely depend on how long you plan to be abroad, as accidents are more likely during longer trips.

Coverage Essentials

Travel insurance companies like Travel Insured International even offer travel insurance online with a variety of coverages for destinations worldwide. What to look for when buying your policy will depend on who you're traveling with, where you're going, and which activities you'll likely be involved in.

Let's look at the five essentials of travel insurance:

Medical Coverage

To acquire any Schengen visa type, you must secure medical insurance of at least 30,000€ valid throughout the Schengen Zone. Medical treatment costs in Europe can be pretty high, so this insurance may be a good fit regardless of where you're coming from. You can also opt for additional coverage if you'd like some extra peace of mind. For more information on this insurance, check out

"International Travel Insurance" with companies such as Europe Assistance or Bupa.

Natural Disaster

If a natural disaster occurs during your travel that delays your trip for the specified number of travelers in your natural disaster insurance plan, will be reimbursed for expenses like accommodations and meals. Severe weather conditions which affect your flights are also valid reasons for filing a claim under this coverage.

Personal Belongings and Documents

While traveling internationally, sometimes things don't go as planned with your documents and personal belongings. Should the worst occur and your luggage gets lost, stolen, or damaged during travel, this will cover your loss.

CFAR (Cancel for Any Reason)

This insurance has you covered if your trip gets canceled (for example, if the flights are suspended or you can't make it to the airport).

IFAR (Interruption for Any Reason)

This coverage kicks in from the moment your trip begins in case you have to interrupt it. So, if a member of your travel group falls ill halfway through the journey, this package will reimburse the costs.

Trip Delay

Never worry again about covering the financial risks related to trip delays caused by third parties!

Selecting the Right Policy

This array of insurance options might leave you feeling a bit dizzy. But don't worry (*non preoccuparti*)! It's normal for different travelers to select different coverages. If getting travel insurance is a must for you, then I recommend purchasing a comprehensive or all-inclusive policy to save you the burden of squinting at the fine print, which comes with purchasing multiple packages from multiple sources. All-inclusive policies may include trip delay, interruption, and cancellation; emergency medical (including medical evacuation and repatriation); and baggage coverage.

Solo Travelers

I strongly recommend looking into insurance packages offering coverages that will help you feel safe when exploring alone. Also, consider coverage that ensures maximum flexibility in accommodating a last-minute change of plans.

Families

Families traveling with children might be interested in coverage that covers all of a child's unique medical needs. Group discounts benefit families traveling in large numbers and are common in a few insurance packages.

Couples

Couples traveling together can opt for combined coverage, which allows them to share all the benefits of an individual insurance package.

Regardless of your choice, it's a good idea to make your purchases at least 21 days after your first payment for your trip (i.e., booking hotels or flights). That way, you can attach any necessary documents to your visa application.

NAVIGATING TRAVEL REQUIREMENTS

The Bel Paese is a core member state of the European Union (as a founding member of the institution in the 1950s). The country is also included in the Schengen Zone, a group of 28 European nations that have jointly agreed to the same visa requirements for third-country nationals. As of the time of writing, the complete list of Schengen

States includes Austria, Belgium, Bulgaria, Czechia, Portugal, Romania, Denmark, Estonia, Finland, France, Germany, Greece, Hungary, Iceland, Italy, Latvia, Liechtenstein, Lithuania, Luxembourg, Malta, the Netherlands, Norway, Poland, Slovakia, Slovenia, Spain, Sweden, and Switzerland. Ireland, Croatia, and Cyprus are EU member countries that may also join the Schengen Zone in the future.

Maybe the word "visa" is causing some nervousness. That's common. But remember—almost 65 million tourists are placed in the same position each year when arranging the correct travel visa. Italy has made the process fairly straightforward as the fifth most visited country based on international tourism arrivals. However, I highly recommend knowing a reasonable amount of time ahead of your trip if you will even need a visa to travel there. This section will take you through some common scenarios, one or more of which will likely apply to you.

VISA-FREE TRAVEL

European Union (EU) citizens have visa-free travel opportunities within the EU's borders, so naturally, they can travel to Italy with an EU passport or other valid travel document without issue.

For stays of up to 90 days, **US citizens** holding US passports valid for at least three months from their intended return date from Italy are not obliged to obtain a visa for tourist or business purposes or airport transfers. They will be considered non-residents. Starting in 2025, all US citizens will need to complete a European Travel Information and Authorisation System (ETIAS) application and receive an ETIAS travel authorization before their trip.

Canadian citizens are not required to obtain an entry visa to travel to the Schengen Zone for stays up to 90 days within a 180-day period. They will also be considered non-residents. Likewise, starting in 2025, they will need to complete an ETIAS application to receive a travel authorization prior to their trip.

The UK is not a part of the Schengen area. Moreover, **UK citizens** won't have the right to freedom of movement in the European Union since the UK officially left the EU on January 31, 2020. However, UK citizens have not been asked for entry visas in Italy until now, and they can continue to travel within the EU's borders until the transition period ends. However, starting in 2025, they'll need ETIAS authorization to travel to Italy and other Schengen Zone countries for stays of up to 90 days in a 180-day period.

Understanding Italy's Visa Types

If you are looking to travel for more than 90 days within the space of 180 days or none of the above nationalities match your passport, then read the following section. Please note that the processing time will take a minimum of *14 business days* from the date your documents are received, so be sure to leave at least three weeks from when you start working on your visa to when you board your plane.

Schengen Visa

Undoubtedly the most popular visa option, the Schengen Visa is a bit different from the first three types listed above. This document allows holders to move freely within the Schengen Zone for stays of up to 90 days within a period of 180 days. This visa is perfect for you if you want to explore more of this Zone, as it enables you to travel within the 28 European countries that are also Schengen states (*see the Navigating Travel Requirements section above for a complete list*). Quite simply, all border controls on this visa are abolished.

Category A Schengen Visa: Airport Transit Visa (Applicable for Tourist Purposes) enables holders to travel within the airport to change flights in the international terminal(s). With this visa, you won't be permitted to leave this area.

Category C Schengen Visa: Single-Entry, Double-Entry, Multiple-Entry (Applicable for Tourist Purposes) The single-entry visa grants a one-time entrance within the Schengen Zone. Double-entry visa holders may travel twice over pre-defined periods. Lastly, the multiple-entry visa allows consecutive visits between 3-5 years *without* exceeding the time constraints. All these visas operate on a short-term basis for stays up to 90 days in periods of 180 days. If you're planning to travel to Italy as part of a more extensive European trip, it's worth opting for this visa type.

Assuming that you have picked up this book intending to visit the Bel Paese as a tourist (or at least for most of your journey), please note that I have not included visas related to work, study, family relations, business, or asylum seekers, nor have I included which visa(s) you may need or their fees and application procedures. If you'll be traveling to Italy for one or more of these purposes, please head over to the website of your nearest Italian Embassy or Consulate to check for updates. Additionally, if you wish to stay longer than you are allowed as a tourist, I strongly recommend researching to find out which visa you'll need.

NAVIGATING CURRENCY

Money is so hard to earn yet so easy to spend. In this section, we'll cover some essentials designed to help you make the most of your Italian adventure.

In February 2002, the EU's single currency—the euro—replaced Italy's old *lira* currency. The euro uses a decimal system of euros and cents, with one euro equaling 100 cents.

There are euro coins in eight denominations: 1 cent, 2 cents, 5 cents, 10 cents, 20 cents, 50 cents, 1€, and 2€. The currency's banknotes are identical across the eurozone and do not have a national design. Each banknote differs in size and color, so each of its seven denominations (5€, 10€, 20€, 50€, 100€, 200€, and 500€) can be easily distinguished. Realistically, you only want to carry the four smaller denominations out and about town to avoid annoying your friendly local market vendor with a 100€ note.

What Can the Euro Buy Me?

It's handy to estimate costs for your trip before you go so you know just how much money to exchange. Remember that you can use the euro anywhere in the EU. Prices vary across Italy, but these are some average costs:

- 110-200€ per night: A double room in a mid-range hotel
- 2.50€: A slice of pizza
- 3€: A bottle of local Italian wine
- 10-20€: A standard museum entry ticket
- 25-45€ Dinner at a local restaurant

HOW TO EXCHANGE CURRENCY IN ITALY

Many Italian restaurants and shops prefer cash, so you should always have a little on hand while you travel. Although it can be a better value to buy the currency before you depart (*see the section on that below*), you can also get it once you arrive in the country. Just alert your card issuer(s) that you'll be traveling so they know your purchases and withdrawals in Italy are legitimate.

ATMs (*bancomat*) and currency exchange outlets (*cambi*) are the most popular ways to get euros in the Bel Paese.

Italian Bank ATMs (Bancomat)

Bancomat are a godsend. Most don't charge the operator fee you see in many other countries. Avoid independent ones, as they may charge hefty fees or be scam machines.

You'll probably have a withdrawal limit of 250–300€ per day. Bancomat have been known to be temperamental with foreign cards, so it's always a good idea to make sure you have some cash on hand at all times.

Italian Currency Exchange Outlets (Cambi)

Cambi are available all over Italy, but the rates and fees vary significantly.

The ones at airports and hotels (anywhere very touristy) will probably offer poor exchange rates, so it's better to wait until you can compare options in town.

Make sure the bills you bring from home are in good condition. Some exchange services reject defaced or damaged currency.

Using Your Bank Card in Italy

Some of the best travel money cards include debit, credit, and prepaid cards. You can use Visa and Mastercard almost everywhere, but American Express isn't accepted as often (and you may pay a higher fee).

Important tip: Watch out for dynamic currency conversion (DCC) when using your bank card. This is where you'll be asked whether you'd like to pay in the local currency or your home currency. *Always choose the local currency!* DCC is well known to provide poor currency conversion rates, and you may pay additional fees for the service.

Prepaid Travel Cards

Traveling with a prepaid travel card is highly recommended, especially when you're still learning the ropes of a new place. Revolut and Wise debit cards can be the perfect options if you're someone who likes to have some currency beforehand so that later on, you can load a prepaid amount onto your card.

Travelers' Checks

Even though it's one of the most visited countries in the world, Italy is not accepting of travelers' checks. So, if you're looking for convenience and better value, it's better to stick with bancomat and cambi.

Buying Italian Currency Before You Go

As I mentioned, it is best to exchange currencies before leaving your home country. Time *is* money, so why waste a second searching for cambi or bancomat when you could be living up your first night in Rome sipping an aperitivo?

The three best ways to save yourself some time by purchasing euros back home are:

- Buying euros online to be delivered or for you to pick up in-store.
- Swapping your home currency for euros at a currency exchange store.
- Getting euros at your bank.

TRAVEL ESSENTIALS AND PACKING TIPS

You've booked your hotel and your flight, and even convinced your traveling companion to take time off work to join you on what will be an incredible Italian adventure. Now what? Packing for the big unknown can be one of the hardest things to do. To help you out, I've compiled a list, which is in no way exhaustive, of smart packing strategies and essentials to help get the ball rolling for this one final step.

Packing Guide for Solo Travelers

Do	Don't
• Use a small suitcase or backpack (preferably multi-purpose)	• Bring any expensive technology that is not backed up first.
• Wear your bulkiest items on travel days	• Bring basic toiletries you can easily buy at cheaper Italian supermarkets (if you're traveling for longer than three weeks)
• Use travel-sized toiletries or soap/shampoo bars	
• Roll your clothes	
• Pack a basic first-aid kit	

Packing Guide for Families

Do (also see Solo Travelers' table)	Don't (also see Solo Travelers' table)
• Keep a copy of your details with each piece of luggage (i.e., name and phone number) in case your items get lost	• Use a separate suitcase for each family member
• Let young children get involved with packing; sometimes, they actually know what's best for themselves!	• Pack everything you think you will need; be intentional and use good judgment
• Use packing cubes; take advantage of the extra space	
• Pack a spare set of children's clothes in your carry-on luggage	
• Pack a basic first-aid kit	
• Scan and email documents to yourself	
• Know your luggage weight and dimension allowances	
• Leave some spare room in your suitcase for gifts and souvenirs	

Packing Guide for Couples

Do (also see the last two tables)

- Share pieces of technology (i.e., Kindles, iPads) to save space, reduce luggage weight, and avoid the possibility of loss

A Side Note on Clothing

Bring light-to-medium-weight clothing and rainwear if you plan on traveling in autumn or early spring.

During winter, you'll be grateful that you brought a warm overcoat for the north and a light overcoat for the south.

For those cooler evenings in May through September, summer clothes made of cotton, linen, or other natural fabrics, along with a jacket or cardigan, should do the job.

Casual wear is generally the norm, but remember to cover up bare backs, arms, midriffs, and short shorts when entering places of worship.

ESSENTIAL ITEMS CHECKLIST

- Small backpack for use as a carry-on
- Water bottle filter
- Microfiber towel
- Packing cubes
- Money pouch RFID (prevents cards from being scanned)
- Padlock (for hostels) and backpack zippers
- Disinfectant wipes
- Shower shoes
- Universal power adapters
- Inflatable neck pillow
- Travel-size shampoo and conditioner bottles

Beyond this checklist, consider which activities you would like to include in your trip (or not) and pack accordingly. Perhaps sitting in the sun all day outside a café sounds like your ideal vacation, so you'll want to pack sunscreen! Just remember—no matter if you're chilling out or heading around town, comfortable walking shoes are indispensable.

NEXT STEPS...

So (*Allora*), I hope the nitty-gritty practicalities of planning your incredible journey are much clearer now. I have tried to be representative rather than exhaustive in my explanations of budgets, suitable accommodation types, travel insurance, visas, currency, and packing essentials. Please use what's best from these offerings for your unique situation as you craft your perfect Italian getaway. But, no matter how you travel, do it with confidence!

It won't be long until your trip now! Soon you'll be receiving all those tearful *buon viaggio* (have a good trip) wishes as you wave goodbye to your daily life at home. As we set out on this adventure together, the chapters to come will unveil the wonders of Italy awaiting you, one by one. So, pack your curiosity—we'll be going over all the details.

That's all well and good, you may be thinking, but how will these surprises be revealed to me? And how can I travel safely? Let's go to Chapter 2 to find out!

CHAPTER 2
EXPLORING ITALY SAFELY

 Qui va piano, va sano (Who Goes Slowly, Goes Safely)

AN OLD ITALIAN SAYING

GETTING AROUND WITH EASE

The Bel Paese is a well-connected country with working high-speed trains, modern highways, domestic flights, and bus and ferry connections. Every Italian adventure should include at least one local mode of transportation if only to get a feel for the "real" Italy. However, knowing the ins and outs of these different systems can be a little tricky at first, so here's a breakdown of ways to get around, including practical tips.

Trains

Europe's primary train ticket platforms–Trainline, Omio, and Rail Europe–will get you on the right track. They are safe and generally easy to navigate. I have used Trainline for years in Italy and other places and have never had an issue finding or booking tickets.

Trainline will also send you news updates on the latest strikes (Trainline, n.d.).

Popular High-Speed Train Networks

Route	Distance	Fastest Journey
Rome–Venice	245 miles (394 km)	3h 16m
Rome–Florence	144 miles (232 km)	1h 17m
Rome–Naples	117 miles (188 km)	1h 07m
Florence–Venice	127 miles (204 km)	2h 01m
Milan–Rome	296 miles (476 km)	3h 10m
Milan–Florence	155 miles (249 km)	1h 44m

(Taken from Trainline's website. Check it for the latest fares.)

By the way, I recommend taking trains only for long-distance journeys from one part of the country to another, like from Naples to Milan. Unless you're a train buff with a lot of time and patience, Italian trains are not to be wholeheartedly trusted, as delays and frequent strikes can (and have) caused many travelers to miss their trips. Sleeping in the station and waiting for the next train to your destination isn't nearly as exhilarating as it sounds...

Private Vehicle Options

Personal Car Rental

Renting a car in Sicily was one of the best decisions I made for a four-day road trip, so I highly recommend this to anyone looking for a more hands-on experience on Italian roads. Most car rental companies are easy to work with and relatively reasonable price-wise. For instance, your standard 5-seat automatic Tesla with a 380-mile (612-km) range can cost you 124€ to rent for four days.

The most breathtaking Italian adventures are found on the road. The *autostrada*, Italy's main highway, runs the length and breadth of the peninsula, making driving the single most convenient way of getting around the country and appreciating its beauty.

It's no secret that Italian drivers have a particular instinct for driving, one many foreigners cannot match. On the road, avoid being reckless or hesitant. Never try to one-up Italian drivers; this will only escalate their competitive spirit. Yet, remember that driving for long periods behind a slowpoke is unforgivable for Italians.

As soon as you pull into a big city, park somewhere safe and convenient without a second thought, and then grab a bus, subway, or tram. Don't even think about driving somewhere built-up like Naples; it'll only welcome the chance of possible (and very frequent) road hazards.

Private Chauffeurs

When needed, it'll be simpler for you to hire private drivers by going through professional travel management agencies such as Taylor Management, which can arrange VIP transportation, private security, and personal itineraries for you throughout your trip. You can get a price quote by messaging or calling them directly.

Uber and Private Drivers

Uber is available only in major cities like Rome and Milan. Just don't expect the Uber you know back home to be the same in Italy. When you order a car on Uber, the app will put you directly in touch with private (one-time hire) drivers called Noleggio Con Conducente (NCC). Currently, tensions are running high regarding the use of Uber in Italy. This is because it's already very complicated to become a registered taxi driver there, independent of joining any third-party rideshare company beyond that. Often, it's best to call a local taxi; you'll be saving money and supporting local drivers. Your host or a local tourist office should also be able to get you in touch with a taxi company they trust.

Airport Transfers

Please see the section above on private drivers if getting to and from the airport by car suits your journey. Airports will vary in their distances from their nearby cities. Take Rome, for example. You can get from the Fiumicino airport to the center of the city in 50 minutes by subway. However, these types of rides will differ for each region. If you're on a budget, consider using a local bus or subway instead of ordering a private car. Usually, there is a tourist information desk in the airport arrival section where you can find more specific information if needed.

Flying Within Italy

Here is another "When in Rome" moment: When flying domestically, naturally, you'll want to use domestic airlines. ITA Airways is one of the most popular airlines, and I recommend them for flights within the country. While browsing, it's best to shift to the Italian language to get a more fluid experience and find the best prices.

Buses

As misleading as the name Trainline suggests, you can also book bus tickets here. If you're traveling long distances, say from Turin to Salerno, Trainline can offer tickets for direct routes for as low as 7€

with companies like FlixBus and MarinoBus. It's worth checking your local tourist desk to find more specific information on everyday public bus transportation in your city.

Ferries

With four marginal seas (all sub-basins of the Mediterranean) bordering the Italian peninsula, it's not a bad idea to travel to the mainland by boat. There are 13 operating ports to sail from or harbor in, including Palermo and Catania in Sicily and Caligari, Olbia, and Porto Torres in Sardinia. Crossing the water from the mainland to these two islands by boat makes good sense and is also a convenient gateway to exploring more of the Mediterranean. If you're traveling on a Schengen visa, try to take advantage of sailing east from the mainland port of Ancona to Split, Croatia, or west from Porto Torres to Barcelona, Spain. These 6-14-hour overnight boat rides present a perfect opportunity to discover the crystal-clear waters of the Mediterranean in all its richness.

SAFETY TIPS FOR ALL TRAVELERS

While it may not be the most exciting of points, learning how to balance risk-taking and staying safe as you travel is extremely important. As we immerse ourselves in a new environment, it is safest to try different experiences within reason.

In 2023, the Global Peace Index rated Italy the 34th most peaceful country out of 163. Rather than political instability or random violent conflicts in public, this statistic reflects the nation's more general challenges regarding petty theft and organized crime. As for crime within the country itself, Statista released a report in 2021 revealing Milan to be the leading province for illegal activity such as petty commercial burglary. Some may speculate that the Lombardic area is more susceptible to crime since it is landlocked and at the cusp of congested borders like France, Switzerland, Austria, Slovenia, and

Croatia. Still, these figures and perceptions are no reason to avoid travel.

Just like moving around any busy city, be vigilant. Traveling as a tourist will undoubtedly make you stand out, so it's best to take extra precautions. However, rest assured that I have always felt safe in all my years of traveling around Bella Italia, either solo or with friends. True, I have had a few possessions stolen, but more often than not, I became the main culprit by mindlessly leaving my things out in the open. Because of me, my possessions were practically screaming, "Take me!"

To help you avoid similar pitfalls, here are some situational non-negotiables to ensure you can navigate safely.

Transportation Safety

Public Transportation

Be cautious when using public transportation and while walking in crowded urban areas. Take particular care in and around main stations like the Termini in Rome, where incidents of street muggings have been reported.

Make sure to keep an eye on your bags at all times when unloading them from coaches and at cruise-ship ports. Also, watch your belongings closely on trains, especially the Circumvesuviana and any that stop at airports.

Theft From Cars

Robberies from parked cars are pretty common, especially in Ostia, Milan, Pisa, and throughout the Colosseum area in Rome. Coastal areas and auto service stations can become excellent targets, so always lock your vehicle, never leave valuables inside, and avoid leaving your luggage in the trunk for any length of time. Roadway robbers may try to distract you or get you to stop your vehicle by seeking help or directions or claiming something is wrong with another vehicle.

Hotel Safety

Most booking websites, such as booking.com, require all their accommodation listings to be verified before connecting them with customers.

If you are booking with an accommodation directly, it's best to search for them online before and then scan their review page and surrounding location. Does the price roughly correspond to the kind of area in which they are located? If you're still worried, call them up. You can often get a better feel for things that way.

It's also best not to have all your essential personal items on you when exploring the Bel Paese. Your hotel will likely have a safe for storing valuables, ID, and money. If not, you may still want to ask the reception to keep these items safe–*only if you feel they are trustworthy.*

Don't Stand Out When Traveling

Nothing is holding you back from dressing up while on your trip; you're on vacation, after all! But again, we return to the classic concept of *balance.* In other words, wear what you feel is reasonable for the moment; just be sure not to overdress and make yourself an attractive mugging target.

Beware of Scams

Italy descends from a long historical lineage of artifice–from the Roman Empire's absorption of the Greek Commedia Dell'arte to the origins of opera in the 17th century. While the glitz and glamor may have their charms, don't let any scams or criminal "comedies (*commedie)*" pull the wool over your eyes.

- **Dress-up Scammers**

As you stroll through busy areas, you may see people dressed up as Roman soldiers or gladiators at the Colosseum. These individuals may seem friendly, beckoning you to take pictures. After taking some for you to post on social media, they will ask you to pay.

- **Pickpockets**

No sensation could be worse than the feeling of fingers sneaking into your back pocket during a crowded rush hour on an equally stuffy public bus. Unfortunately for my rogue friend, he didn't find anything of value there except a small lip balm, which I would have been more than willing to give him if he genuinely needed it. In all seriousness, do your best to avoid these incidents, especially on public transportation. Pickpockets often operate in pairs–one who distracts you while the other slips their fingers into your pocket. Beware of bag snatching, too. So, zip up bags (padlock them if you need extra peace of mind) and hide all your valuables well.

- **Fake Luxury Products**

These setups are not limited to Italy. An experienced globetrotter will probably have seen people selling "luxury" bags and tacky designer shades in cities worldwide. In this case, yes, it *is* too good to be true. These items are most definitely plastic and fake.

- **Rose Scam**

This one's a bit similar to our gladiator friends in Rome. Rose scammers like to approach unsuspecting tourists sitting in outside cafés, where they will gently place a single rose on the table. If you are that tourist and don't wish to purchase a rose for the lover sitting across from you, *do not* pick it up, however sweet you imagine its scent. The scammer will try to charge you for simply touching the flower.

- **Unofficial Street Tours**

Be on the lookout for unqualified tour guides. Where the flow of tourists increases, so do the ranks of scammers on the hunt for the next jackpot. Please don't give them that chance. If you want to book a tour, book it with a trusted guide; a stranger on the street corner is likely a fraud.

- **Overpriced Taxis**

Not all taxi drivers in the Bel Paese are dishonest–far from it (sadly, the unscrupulous few give the others a bad rep). Still, be cautious; running into the wrong cabs is easy once you emerge from the airport or train station's arrival gates after a long journey. Trust me; some will be waiting willingly. Signs to look out for in these situations include the driver not turning the meter on, claiming that they only take cash (by Italian law, they need to be able to accept cards), and returning incorrect change (i.e., you hand over a 50-euro note, and they give you back 10 when they should have given you back 20). Also, before you agree to a ride, have a rough idea of what the fare should really be. Without knowing this, you run the risk of being taken advantage of with rates that are higher than the standard. For instance, the fare between the airport and the city center in Rome should be around 50€.

- **Fake Car Crash**

If you've mustered the courage to hit the road, be on the lookout for the so-called "mirror scam." Known as the *truffa dello specchietto*, this trick begins with a loud noise that's actually made with a rock or piece of wood. Believing that their "reckless" driving has caused third-party damage, drivers will pull over, only to be approached by a stranger who falsely accuses them of causing damage to another's vehicle. The evidence will be brought forward to reveal an already-cracked side mirror (or something similar), leaving the stunned driver (often foreign) no option but to hand over reparations in cash to the criminals.

- **Ticket Helpers**

At train stations, the swarms of people going in every direction imaginable can be dizzying. Keep your wits about you. Ideally, you'll have entered the station already furnished with your tickets (preferably digitized). If this is not the case, and you have to print them out at self-service, *do not* let anyone help you. Some scammers will try to help you navigate the platform, and not for free, mind you. A tip is *always* expected.

If anything feels strange, trust your gut instinct and do not proceed. Kindly refuse any offer and calmly move away from the situation.

STRIKES AND DEMONSTRATIONS

One of the first words you must memorize as soon as you step on Italian soil is strike (sciopero). Strikes are far more common there than in other parts of the world, but they can be surprisingly stress-free when you know how to handle them. Keep your eyes and ears open for news of a strike. Most of the time, they'll be announced about one week before they happen. What's the easiest way to stay informed? Just ask at your hotel reception desk. Otherwise, check the screens at bus or train stops for details on any planned strikes. If you're in Rome, upcoming news of transportation strikes will also appear on the website of ATAC, the main public transportation provider there. Each Italian city will have its own equivalent. It's also worth checking the website of the primary Italian train operator, Trenitalia. Familiarize yourself with other strike-related vocabulary words like those for a demonstration (*manifestazione/dimostrazione*) since demonstrations also often affect public transportation. If you see "suspended" (*sospeso* or *sospesa*) on the board at train stations, it means that you're looking at a suspended line.

TERRORISM

In this troubled political climate, it shouldn't be surprising that Italy has upped its terrorist alert level. The government has advised the population to remain vigilant at all times, and the authorities will increase security, for example, around major Jewish communities when there is conflict in the Middle East. Given the increased global tensions, I can't rule out the possibility of a terrorist attack totally. The best you can do is to stay aware of your surroundings, stay away from demonstrations, and follow the advice of local officials.

LAWS AND CULTURAL DIFFERENCES

Personal ID

Always be prepared to show identification to the authorities if they ask to see it. Most of the time, they will accept a photocopy of your passport, but may also ask to see a second form of photo ID. The police usually request to see your original passport if you are driving and they pull you over.

Public Transportation

You'll need to validate your bus or train tickets using a ticket machine before beginning your journey. Two hours into my first trip to Italy, I learned this the hard way. Inspectors regularly patrol public transport and will issue an on-the-spot fine of 100–500 euros (which can be graciously reduced to 50 euros if paid immediately) if you lack a validated ticket.

Tourist Tax

Many Italian cities charge a nominal tourist tax. You'll pay this at your hotel in addition to the price you're charged for any packages or prepaid arrangements. The tax amount will depend on the city you're in and the star rating of your hotel. As a rough sketch, a 2.50€ per night tourist tax will be asked from each person staying in a three-star hotel. Hotels often ask for payment in cash, so make sure you get a receipt. For more information, check with the local tourist information office. You may also need to pay an access fee if you visit Venice. More information on this can be found on the Venice City Hall website.

Emergency Numbers to Know in Italy

Should you ever need help, don't hesitate to dial...

- #112 for Emergencies in Europe–free of charge and open 24/7 anywhere in the European Union. This number will give access to the fire department, police, or ambulance services.
- #118 for direct communication with medics if you need any health-related assistance. Also use this number for mountain or cave rescues.
- #113 for direct communication with police.
- #115 for direct communication with the fire department. This number can also be used in weather emergencies.
- #803.116 for Roadside Assistance–toll-free when dialed from a landline or mobile phone with an Italian provider, open 24/7. This service is provided by the Automobile Club d'Italia (ACI), an organization of 106 local clubs that advocate for Italian drivers.
- #1515 for forest rangers.
- #1518 for travel information.
- #1530 for sea rescue.

Minimize Risks By:

- Digitizing important documents
- Avoiding packing valuables

- Booking travel insurance
- Carrying a scanned copy of your passport
- Safeguarding your hotel room
- Avoiding the use of public WiFi, which prevents hackers from stealing your data
- Being aware of scammers
- Being aware of your surroundings
- Drinking responsibly, especially when by yourself
- Keeping in touch with family and friends
- Bringing and using travel padlocks
- Knowing the local emergency info
- Learning the local lingo
- Planning your accommodation
- Planning your itinerary and researching your destinations
- Avoiding oversharing online
- Avoiding traveling alone at night

SAFETY FOR SOLO TRAVELERS

It's been a long day, and you already have so much to reflect on. Italy's streetlights and classic architecture illuminate the path back to your hotel. While the pavement is well-lit and relatively lively, you realize that your peace of mind is slowly giving way to thoughts of panic. Your fingers itch to clutch your bag, which you realize you left open after paying at the restaurant. In a flurry, you dive in headfirst, scrambling around inside it to check that you still have your wallet, cash, and ID, which are there just as you left them. The tightness in your chest loosens as you let out a sigh of relief.

It's nothing to be embarrassed about—we all run into those palm-on-face moments. Plus, it can be challenging to stay focused on little things like zipping wallets and bags—especially backpacks we don't always have an eye on—when traveling alone. Without an extra pair of eyes watching our things, solo travelers like us need to be even more vigilant when it comes to staying safe. This is why picking the safest, most reliable accommodations is paramount, as the people there will be your first point of contact if there are any problems. The best thing you can do is to be as frank as possible at the reception desk (if you feel they are trustworthy). Be upfront about your situation and let them know you might need them during your visit. More often than not, they'll be thrilled to help you out.

Further Actions You Can Take

Still looking for more advice? Here are some additional tips:

Before You Travel:

- **Plan Your Transportation**

You can learn more about transportation options online or from your hotel, a local Italian tourist office, or a close friend.

- **Be Aware of Your Mental Health**

Open up to a family member, trusted friend, or even your therapist about your plans and possible worries about traveling alone. You can think through strategies together to combat feelings of anxiety and loneliness that might arise. It's always best to build a solid support network, even if they are far away.

- **Tell People Where You're Going**

After discussing your travel plans with friends and family, it's a good idea to let them know where you'll be going and when you'll be there. You might feel even more comfortable sharing your host's contact details with those in your trusted circle—just in case!

- **Make An Emergency Plan**

Memorize the emergency numbers in this chapter in case you need them. Think about the city layout, too. Take some time, perhaps on the first and second day of your trip to a city, to become familiar with the area, including the nearest hospital and police station.

While You're Traveling:

- **Choose Safe Transportation**

It's handy to plan your trip from the airport to your hotel–or at least the center of the city or town where you'll be staying–before you even land. This can be easily done through your hotel or host.

- **Be Safe in Your Accommodation**

Keep valuables that you won't need daily in your room safe or at a trusted reception desk. If you feel anything is out of order, bring this up with your host.

- **Be Safe While You're Out and About**

Knowing which areas are off-limits is critical. If you're in Naples, for example, avoid neighborhoods like Scampia (respectfully). Potentially dangerous places like this have little to offer unwitting tourists.

- **Socialize Safely**

Being kind and striking up a cheerful, appropriate conversation should never invite danger, though sometimes it may turn out that way. If you feel someone is crossing your boundaries, leave immediately, and if you can't, defuse the situation by cutting off the conversation and getting away.

SAFETY CONSIDERATIONS FOR WOMEN

It's important to restate that most Italian criminal activity revolves around petty theft and organized crime confined to local daily life. With this in mind, it is also a hugely popular travel destination, with millions upon millions visiting to soak up the peninsula's sun and spirit each year.

No matter where in the country you're traveling, the key to ensuring personal safety is staying street-smart and planning ahead.

Safety By Night

Although I've been lucky enough never to run into a significant issue while going out in Italy, many problems I've consistently heard from friends (both local and foreign) and family members have almost always pertained to the nightlife there. While cat-calling, wolf-whistles, and uncalled-for staring are regretfully seen as the norm in public, most of the riskier situations for women occur after hours.

I've heard stories from women traveling alone and in pairs about the unpleasantness of using public transportation at night. Being constantly on the lookout when drinking at bars and clubs is also a given. Because the portions of alcohol are often much more generous than you might be used to, be prepared to drink responsibly. This information is in no way intended to dampen your fun, but just be cautious, particularly when alcohol is involved. To avoid your drink being spiked, take it with you to the restroom if you're clubbing alone, and never leave it unattended, nor entrust it to someone you've just met. It's best not to risk leaving it with a bartender in a busy local club, either, because you just never know.

If you're partying, try not to stay out alone until the early hours of the morning. Instead, consider buddying up with other people you trust. It's always safest to hang out with larger groups.

Other Tips to Consider When Going Out:

• **Use Taxis and Rideshares Safely**

Ready to go home? Avoid calling a cab from the street corner late at night. My advice is to have a trusted taxi company number (*see the earlier section on safe private car travel*) saved in your phone contacts so all you need to do is dial and be ready to leave. Another good move is to speak to your host about the taxi services they recommend.

• **Look Like You Know Where You're Going**

This will come naturally once you've scouted your location and feel more confident there. For this reason, it may be a good idea to leave those clubbing nights for a little later on in the trip. Likewise, research your destination and its surrounding area online. Is it safe to go to in the first place? What are the travel options for the ride back?

• **Leave Your Valuables at Home**

Do you really need to carry two forms of ID and wear three blingy necklaces when you're dancing? Before leaving your accommodation, think twice about taking valuables with you. Decide which ones will really be useful and which ones to leave behind.

• **Use Your Phone Strategically**

Petty theft is common in Italy. Cruising down a road you're unfamiliar with late at night after you've had a couple of drinks is not recommended, especially if your brand-new smartphone is flashing all over the place. Use your phone to help you get your bearings, and then try to keep it tucked away in a safe place as much as possible.

- **Buy a Local SIM Card**

Traveling solo means you'll have to rely on your phone, whether it's for maps, contacts, or a translation app. To save yourself from ending up in the middle of nowhere with no means of safe communication, buy a local SIM card. This will help you avoid high roaming costs, being out of range of a WiFi hotspot, running out of credit, or having specific phone calls blocked. What's more, a portable charger can work wonders, so invest in one!

- **Join Solo Female Traveler Groups**

The power of social media comes into play here. If you're feeling super adventurous, check out groups on your favorite apps and websites. The key here is to avoid ending up alone in an unfamiliar place after hours.

- **Don't Be Afraid to Get Loud**

Someone just crossed your boundary? If you feel it is safe to do so, trust your instincts and call it out. Inappropriate behavior in any context is wrong and should always be challenged. I would only do this if I were in an establishment like a bar, restaurant, or shop. Voicing your complaint to the management should be your first move. However, I would not do this in other places, like a dim, deserted street, since it might escalate the issue.

- **Share Your Location with Someone You Trust**

I got this tip from my old roommate at college. Whenever I went on one of my trips to Europe, she would constantly pester me to share my location with her, just in case. At the time, I thought she was just being overprotective, but after running into situations where I've gotten lost abroad and have had to panic-call her, I've had a total change of heart. Having local support at the ready has also put me at ease while traveling solo.

- **Drink Moderately and at a Slower Pace**

I never used to like carrying things when going out to dinner or clubbing. But the day before I'd planned to go out dancing (on the fourth or fifth day of the two weeks I'd planned to visit Milan), I called my best friend back home. We talked for ages, and of course, I told her about my plan to brave it and go to a club on my own for the first time. She was obviously excited for me, but one of the first things she told me to do was bring my own flask of water, conveniently colored neon green. "No," she said, "Don't risk buying a plastic bottle which you're only going to get mixed up with all the other ones. Just bring your own wacky bottle!" I didn't warm up to her idea at first, but now, looking back, I'm so glad I had it so I could get by on fewer cocktails and drink them more slowly. I didn't need to get wasted to have fun, and besides, I had way more peace of mind, which allowed me to stay present and fully enjoy the evening.

- **Spend Extra Money on Staying Safe**

It's understandable to worry about your budget, especially when traveling alone. But look at it this way: If your choice is between getting that cute top or ordering a cab in the middle of the night to get back to your accommodation safely, then suddenly, the decision doesn't seem so hard anymore.

- **Solidarity Outside the Stalls**

Whenever I've gone out to music venues at home or abroad, the most solidarity I've felt is outside the stalls in the female restroom. Honestly, it might sound strange to some, but retreating into this space for a quick timeout often leads to chilled-out conversations with other women.

Once, I was out listening to live music in a bar in Milan and had been vaguely conscious of a guy giving me strange looks from the moment I walked in. I wouldn't have felt so anxious if this were happening back home, but I wasn't familiar with this new city yet. About an hour into the gig, the man was *still* looking at me, dipping in and out of conversation with his friend group. I desperately wanted to leave but would have felt uncomfortable walking out alone. I ducked into the ladies' room for a time-out and was so glad I did! I quickly got to chatting with a local Milanese girl who spoke perfect English, and told her my anxieties about what was happening out there. She completely understood and invited me to join her and her sister at their table. That small interaction turned my night around completely. I got to stay and listen to some great music—as I'd planned— and made some new connections, too.

If you glean anything from these anecdotes, I hope it's how important it is to stay assertive while enjoying your you-time in Bella Italia to the fullest!

LGBTQIA+ TRAVELER SAFETY INSIGHTS

The LGBTQIA+ Community encompasses a spectrum of individuals who self-identify either as Lesbian, Gay, Bisexual, Transgender, Queer or Questioning, Intersex, or Asexual, as well as those whose identities go beyond such labels.

Without mincing words, life for Queer people in Italy has been recently complicated by the country's inauguration of right-wing politician and prime minister Giorgia Meloni. Sadly, the policies represented by Meloni's government have been far from affirming for marginalized social groups.

While generally accepting of LGBTQIA+ people, the country still has a long way to go to incorporate individuals from the Community into its laws. While same-sex relationships are legal and mostly accepted, same-sex marriage is currently not legal. This is, however, the complicated reality of most Christian churches worldwide, so it is not confined to the Italian nation. According to a report released by Statista in 2020, although over 90% of Italians formally belong to the Catholic Church, the results of a recent survey indicate that only 25% of respondents defined their relationship to the Church as "traditional"–a term which has long carried prejudicial baggage, particularly against women's liberation and LGBTQIA+ rights. Anti-discrimination laws are present in the workplace, yet few formal laws have been passed to protect sexual orientation or gender identity in other life contexts, such as the education system.

The diversity in social groups always brings out various nuances. Travelers exploring popular destinations like Milan, Venice, Florence, and Rome can freely express themselves without any hassle. However, in rural regions, visibly Queer individuals and couples might sense a conservative and less accepting atmosphere. Generally, the north is more accepting of Queerness compared to the south. Nonetheless, there is a growing acceptance of LGBTQIA+ individuals in popular southern tourist spots like Capri in Campania and Taormina in Sicily.

Understanding Local Dynamics

Decoding any possible underlying dynamics is not new in any way for members of the LGBTQIA+ Community; it's what many of us experience every day. The reality is often unpredictable, and experiences can vary depending on your travel situation. For example, the challenges I faced while solo traveling as a visibly Queer woman were so different from the ones my partner and I have faced over the past few years while traveling together. I would be lying if I told you I knew how to deal with every possible tricky situation in Italy. The truth is that I'm still learning. What I *can* guarantee you, however, is a candid account of how my experiences have shaped the ways I have navigated the Queer scene—and let me tell you, it is very much alive and kicking! I'll be diving into more details on Italian Queer culture in Chapter 6.

Choosing LGBTQIA+ Friendly Accommodations

Selecting the best accommodation for you should always be a top priority. As a Queer traveler, there are some features you'll want to look for in a hotel when abroad:

- Check the location. Make sure your hotel is well-situated within the city. The further you branch out from popular areas, the harder it will be to find your bearings, which could become dangerous.
- If possible, verify your hotel's equal rights policy online.

Safety Tips for LGBTQIA+ Couples

Traveling with your romantic partner should be filled with joy, and in the end, the highs and lows of the adventures you share become life-long memories. For some couples, exploring new environments in all their beauty and complexity is a fundamental component of living life as two individuals who are fully committed to each other.

To ensure you and your partner have the most positive experience together in the Bel Paese, consider these tips:

Know The Law

As charming as it can be, recently, the country has, unfortunately, had a more conservative government. Just one example of this regretful transformation has been the 2023 ban on surrogacy, which has been perceived as a clear attack on LGBTQIA+ families by making it harder for Queer couples to have children and protect their rights as parents. Civil unions between same-sex couples became legal in 2016, yet the issue of marriage is still undergoing many heated debates.

My advice for those traveling solo or with a partner is to stay as safe as possible by doing some research to prepare for their trip. The International Lesbian, Gay, Bisexual, Trans, and Intersex Association (ILGA) is a great place to start.

Research Your Accommodation

Going back to basics and picking up or researching LGBTQIA+ magazines like *The Advocate* or *Curve* is an easy way to scout out suitable accommodations. The real game-changer, however, is to get in touch with the hosts themselves. Hotels are often the most popular accommodation option during travel, but finding LGBTQIA+-owned accommodations like B&Bs, for example, makes the experience a whole lot easier to manage.

Pinpoint LGBTQIA+ Hotspots

Knitted within Italy's cultural fabric, there will always be communities that are more accepting. Some may involve more searching to discover (*for some great ideas, head over to Chapter 6*). Cities like Milan and Rome are widely considered the heart and soul of Italian Queer culture. While this, of course, is not entirely true, larger cities will undoubtedly be more likely to host Queer-affirming networks, so whip out your social media and scroll until you've mapped out at least five beacons of safety, like bookstores, bars, and cafés. While you're at it, another tip on social media is to follow LGBTQIA+ travel bloggers and journalists; they usually publish articles outlining the essentials of how to stay connected.

Carry Identification

ID cards are necessary for any traveler, but should a situation arise for those who identify as trans, genderqueer, or gender-nonconforming, having required identification on hand can be lifesaving. Even though the process may seem arduous, make sure before leaving home that your passport and driver's license match your gender identity. This will also speed up the visa process if your journey requires one.

Follow Cultural Cues

Always judge the social climate. Maybe you and your partner have encountered some type of bias or microaggression in a city where you know homosexuality is legal and widely accepted. In cases like this, speaking up and reasserting safe boundaries would probably be reasonable.

Yet, in places where homosexuality is legal but less tolerated, it might be wiser to leave strangers in the gray area about your relationship. It isn't any of their business, and you don't have any responsibility to spell anything out to them. My advice here isn't to "shuffle back into the closet" or "deny who you are," but instead, it's to "negotiate with your surroundings." For example, you and your partner might get talking to a friendly market vendor who offers to throw an extra bunch of tomatoes into your grocery purchase. Perhaps he gets the wrong idea and misinterprets your same-sex relationship to be merely platonic. If this is the case and you still want to peruse the market, then maybe after a side glance or two, to keep yourselves safe, you both agree not to correct him and to avoid canoodling.

Following cultural cues requires you and your partner to be on the same page. Both of you should agree on a plan in advance on how best to respond to any unforeseen intolerance. For instance, if someone accosts or verbally abuses you on the street, it is often safer to disengage. On the other hand, if, for example, you find yourselves stuck on a boat trip and can't get off to get away from homophobic passengers, try to find a more secluded part of the ship where you won't be disturbed and be sure to file a complaint with the management.

Wield Your Wallet

Are you being ignored or treated rudely? No second thought is needed–leave. Do not pay. You know you deserve better than to pay good money for disrespectful customer service. No matter the context, always report the situation to management. If there's no way of getting a refund, write a review of your experience in a measured voice on a customer review website or social media. This has nothing to do with trying to bring about shame. Instead, it has everything to do with standing up for yourself by calling out homophobia so that it's visible to other travelers, some of whom may be vulnerable to falling into a similar situation.

In summary, it's not easy being in a new environment as a Queer traveler, solo or partnered. Remember that while the news can inflate tensions, sometimes just getting to know a city and its people one-on-one can actually surprise you for the better. Law and culture don't always entirely uphold the other's values. Stay aware of your surroundings and make safe, reasonable judgments together with your partner if you're traveling as a couple. If you feel like a situation is breaching your boundaries, know that you never have to put up with it, and while you may not be able to take certain actions, like being extremely vocal, you can always walk away. And to all you wonderful Allies out there–if you ever come across homophobia and you feel it is safe to intervene, then do so. Yes, standing up for your fellow humans may not radically shift prejudicial views, but it can and will reinforce the sense of solidarity on which we all rely.

FAMILY-FRIENDLY SAFETY MEASURES

School's out, officially marking the ideal getaway time for you and your family. All over the world–with some based in Bella Italia itself–friends of mine check in to update me on their latest adventures with their kids. When I mentioned I was going to be writing a guide section for parents traveling with their children, our phone calls lengthened. They were all too pleased to spill the beans on the various hacks they'd discovered firsthand. It goes without saying that travel is highly personal and that whatever works for one family may not work for another. As always, you may treat these tips as guidelines rather than non-negotiables.

Plan, Plan, Plan

The most common advice I received from my 12 parent friends (the majority of whom are between 26 and 35) is that outlining the trip's priorities with your partner from the moment you agree on a destination is vital. Everything will depend on your itinerary, which must consider your children's ages as well as the kinds of experiences your family wants. Crack this code, and choosing the best accommodation for your family will be much easier.

Kid-Friendly Accommodations

Travel is already no picnic when it comes to finding the right places to stay, so throwing a few under-tens into the mix won't exactly simplify the process either, says one friend of mine, a single mother of two little ones whom we'll call Amanda.

Amanda (who often travels to Italy with the kids to visit extended family) says the difference between city and countryside accommodations can be huge, not only because of different amenities and activities but also because of transportation needs like rental cars.

When Booking You and Your Children's Stays in Italian Cities, Consider...

Hotels Over Apartments

A hotel offers plenty to help keep you off your feet so you can enjoy your vacation. You'll find that hotel services will make your everyday parenting duties less intense so that you can actually rest! For anyone who likes the sound of relying on the front desk or concierges for questions and advice, hotel accommodations trump all. Remember the opportunity for room service, too! Of course, the downside can sometimes be a lack of privacy and higher costs for families of four or more, even at a modest two-star hotel. Besides, many hotels are well-equipped to cater to your family's needs, from cribs to high chairs. Just make sure the equipment is reserved as part of the confirmation.

Connecting Rooms and Suites

To truly benefit from downtime, finding hotel rooms with connecting rooms or suites for multiple people with a door between the living room and bedroom is a small but vital hack to remember. This feature, however, may not be so clearly advertised, and will usually require an email or phone call to confirm.

Location, Location, Location

Some days might feel like a total struggle just to get everyone's shoes on and make it out the door, and that's without having to spend even more time dealing with transportation issues. A well-situated accommodation with things to do and see in the immediate area will save you the extra hassle of shuttling everyone over long stretches. Especially with younger children, staying within a five-minute walk of a park or playground can be refreshing and offer much-needed relief. Be sure to make a list of desired activities and confirm that your family will have relatively easy access to them.

Elevators

When considering an apartment, it's also important to remember the physical demands that could pose, especially if you have young children, are traveling with strollers, or have mobility issues. Keep in mind that in Europe, the "first floor" is often one flight up the stairs, and elevators may not be available in some buildings, which would be a challenge if your room were several flights up.

When You're Looking for Accommodations a Little Farther Away from the City, Consider...

Resorts Over Apartments and Villas

All-inclusive resort packages have you covered and let your kids run a little bit wilder. Food, drinks, and, in some cases, entertainment activities are all taken care of, so no one has to worry about the extra cost for that second, third, or fourth serving of food. Stand-alone apartments and villas may have amenities like swimming pools, but you usually have to leave the property for structured entertainment. Not only do resort properties offer the convenience of onsite services, but they also have a lively social atmosphere and offer places like a pool or beach bar where children and families can gather. If you want more privacy and independence, an apartment or small villa would be the preferred choice. Larger villas are ideal for extended families or two families traveling together.

Location, Location, Location

You don't have to struggle–if you'll have a driver or a rental vehicle, make a list of the top sites you'll want to see in Italy and select a property within a 1.5-hour drive.

Space to Play

I'll never get over Amanda's expression as she recalled the moment when her kids got a bit too playful on the freshly mowed lawn of the four-star resort they'd been staying at in Capri. "It was supposed to be my family's downtime," she'd said–one week of bliss away from the busyness of extended family on the mainland. Where there was grass, Amanda's little ones let loose; all the while, mom got a bit of me-time sunbathing only a short distance away. As kids will be kids, Amanda's four-and-six-year-olds did not know that this pristinely cut and pruned garden was not meant for playing around in and that doing so there is actually deeply frowned upon. "Sometimes it's better to ask about the layout to avoid any possible embarrassment," Amanda noted as she spared me the awkward details of that unfortunate afternoon.

A Welcoming Attitude

Luckily for Amanda, her story didn't end so badly. While she was mortified that her children had trampled all over the resort's blooming bougainvillea flowers in their play, she was surprised by the management's calm, understanding, and practical approach. At that point, all she could do was apologize for her kids and offer to reimburse the hotel, whose managers graciously refused all her offers to pay.

Navigating Crowded Spaces

This is always the biggest question I have for my parent friends: How to deal with moving around crowded spaces on vacation? Bella Italia is always busy, even outside its peak summer season. Some tips for navigating the hustle and bustle with young children:

Make Sure They Have Your Phone Number

Calmly discuss with your children the worst-case scenario of their being separated from you if one of you gets lost. Then make sure they always have your cell phone number (including international code if needed) in some form on their person. I have one friend who has his child keep his business card in their pocket in case they need to ask a trustworthy adult to call on their behalf. I've heard of some parents who have their kids wear a bracelet with the number or who even write it on their child's arm with a marker. Other parents I know with children who are old enough for a phone believe that the best thing to do is attach the kids' phones to them with a phone lasso or chain so that some means of communication is always available.

Memorize Their Outfits

Bright, memorable colors create great vacation vibes and offer peace of mind while your family moves through busy areas. Memorize what they are wearing by taking their picture (caps and hats are always helpful). This will also help if you ever need a photo of them to show the authorities. Please make sure they remember what you've got on, too!

Tell Them to Stay Calm and Stay Put

My parents taught me as a child that if we ever got separated, the best thing to do would be to stay calm and stay put in the place where we were last together. This way, you and your child both know where to meet. If your child is of the right age and disposition, tell them to stay put in that spot until you or an adult you're traveling with comes to get them.

Teach Them to Find a Mom

Building on the last point, my parent friends and I agree that even in foreign places, it's safe for your child to find and approach another mom for help in these situations. Other moms will know the sheer panic of traveling with kids and will generally stay calm and stay put with your child until you're reunited with them.

Practice, Practice, Practice

Practice makes perfect. Get your children to repeat the "stay calm, stay put" scenario back to you. Ask them whenever you travel: "What would you do if you got lost? Who would you ask for help? What would you say to her?" Hopefully, they'll never need to do these things, but if they do, at least they'll be ready.

Quick Tips for Emergency Preparedness for Families

Create an Emergency Plan

If and when the unforeseen arises, having a well-thought-out emergency plan can help ensure your family's safety. Consider different event sequences and how best to react. You can also make a checklist of essential emergency contacts–those you've shared your travel plans with both at home and at your destination.

Research Your Destination

Know the weather conditions, local customs, culture, and some basic words in Italian before embarking on your trip. This will keep you one step ahead of risk by ensuring that you pack the clothing you'll need and then plan your activities accordingly.

Pack a First-Aid Kit

A basic first aid kit should include adhesive tape, bandages, gauze pads, burn gel, and antiseptic. These items will help you treat cuts, scrapes, and other minor wounds. Additionally, bring pain relievers you trust and use as directed to alleviate headaches, muscle aches, and other minor ailments. If you have any prescription meds, carry a copy of your prescription(s) just in case.

The Emergency Travel Kit

A kit with essential supplies can make a huge difference in an emergency. This kit goes a little further than your basic first aid to include non-perishable items like granola bars, trail mixes, powdered drink mixes, emergency water pouches, and either water treatment tablets or a small portable water filtration system. Also, to attract attention, consider including lightweight emergency light sticks (which don't require batteries) or a whistle.

Research Local Emergency Services

Knowing and having these key numbers ready will give you greater peace of mind. (*See the previous section on emergency numbers.*)

Learn About the Hidden Survival Tools in Your Car

Traveling by car comes with many perks. Some of them could even be life-saving! In an emergency, your vehicle can do so much more than just transport you from point A to point B. Here's what it offers:

- Shelter: This is obvious, but it is worth mentioning nonetheless. Your car can usually provide adequate protection. Only a warm building is better.
- Light: Use your headlights to illuminate your environment, signal for help, etc.
- Water: If you're in a moist environment, your car provides tools for collecting rain or melting snow into drinkable water.

You can use the hubcaps, cover for the steering wheel, or even the removable cupholders!

- Power: With a full gas tank and a functioning battery, your car can easily power up multiple phones or laptops.
- Radio: Some experts say that information from a radio is more important than food and water. Use your car radio to keep track of local conditions and rescue operations.

Learn the Preparedness Profile of Your Hotel

Most hotels have specific emergency plans to safeguard staff and clients. If you feel a bit worried, it's always best to ask about their procedures for fire/gas leak evacuations and other emergencies.

Set Yourself Up for Safety

Make sure your trusted family members and friends are aware of your travel plans. Being safe also means traveling with devices that work, so bring a portable charger, buy an Italian SIM card, and don't tempt thieves who would jump at any chance to steal your valuables.

Although things might not always go as planned, having a positive attitude, clear head, and emergency preparedness plan will ensure you and your children stay safe in the face of the unexpected. The main thing to remember as a parent is that you're not alone. Plenty of parents experience mishaps. Just remember to let go and enjoy quality time with your family–at least 90% of the time!

NEXT STOP...

Smooth transportation options? Check. General travel safety advice? Also, check. I have attempted to be as frank as possible when going over the nuances inherent in the Italian social climate today, as we've discussed several possible issues specific to those traveling solo, as female-presenting, openly Queer, or as a family. All of this, of course, is a mere simplification of experience, so I would urge you not to let the experiences of another completely dictate the course of your own journey, which is for you to write. As you read the lines engraved on the map of Bella Italia, the routes curve out ahead of you, waiting to be traced and deciphered. Where might the winds take you? Perhaps to some of the country's lesser-known destinations, which we'll be covering in the next chapter!

CHAPTER 3

UNLOCKING ITALY'S HIDDEN TREASURES

> *Italy owes to you an undertaking which has merited the applause of the universe.*

GIUSEPPE GARIBALDI, 1860

This quote by the legendary freedom fighter still sends shivers when read over 150 years after national unification. His eloquent appeal is undoubtedly the noblest place to set off from as you travel across both space and time. Were it not for the Risorgimento (Rising Again) movement for independence, championed by figures like Garibaldi and his supporters, the Italy we're so attached to today would look very different.

What you'll see below is by no means exhaustive (nor exhausting!); the adventure will *always* go on. These parts of the Bel Paese, each with their hidden beauty, have indeed "merited the applause of the universe," if only because their vibrancy has withstood countless tests of time. Newcomers, welcome (*benvenuto!*)! You'll certainly have plenty to choose from.

REGIONS AND CITIES OVERVIEW

From top to toe, the country's boot-shaped peninsula has been divided into 20 administrative regions. To make things more manageable, you can mentally divide the country into four parts: the north, the center, the south, and the islands. For the sake of simplicity, I have organized this overview into similar geographic sections. We'll begin with the regions and then zoom in on the main cities and capitals of each.

The Northwest

Aosta Valley

The country's smallest region, the Aosta Valley, covers only 1,988 square miles (5,149 square kilometers) and borders France, Switzerland, and the Piedmont region. It is also the least densely populated, with a small community of 130,000 inhabitants, many of whom speak a French patois, Valdôtain. Not only is the Aosta Valley picturesque, but it borders the highest mountain in Europe–Mont Blanc. Known as the "Rome of the Alps," the capital city, Aosta, is filled with heavy Roman influences. The amphitheater, Porta Praetoria, is definitely worth a visit. To immerse yourself in the region's authentic culture, consider pairing this with a tour along the mystical San Martino bridge during the festival there in February.

Piedmont

The clue is in the name. Derived from a Latin word meaning "at the foot of the mountain," Piedmont is situated at the very foothills of the Alps on the upper basin of the river Po. This area is in many ways closer in spirit to France than Italy. A glance at the classical Royal Palace (Palazzo Reale) and adjoining Royal Gardens–designed by the same architect as the Versailles Palace of Louis XIV–highlights Gallic ties in Piedmont's stronghold and capital city, Turin.

Turin is best known for its booming industry, most notably the nation's pride and glory: the Fiat auto factory. However, if you think all you'll find here is that and a couple of well-trimmed gardens, think again. Instead, Piedmontese urban planning, with its main streets, squares, and monuments, lends the area an unshakable sense of dignity and panache.

Liguria

This is the vacationer's favorite. Sandy beaches and secluded sun-traps line the Ligurian Coast, dotted every now and then with family resorts. The Italian Riviera, which once boasted an illicit reputation for piracy, gradually faded as its illustrious port city capital, Genoa, rose to prominence. With shady traders under closer watch, this Mediterranean hub looked safer and more promising. You can read part of its history in its sweeping architecture, from St. Matthew's Square (Piazza San Mateo)–the medieval family home of Genoa's patron aristocracy–to the Renaissance and Baroque palaces on Garibaldi Street (Via Garibaldi).

For the full Ligurian experience, chase the sun from Genoa's more rugged east coast on the Riviera of the Rising Sun (Riviera di Levante) all the way west to the Riviera of the Setting Sun (Riviera di Ponente).

Lombardy

When a squadron of Lombards set out from their homes in Eastern Europe to cross the Alps during the Middle Ages, they conquered this central part of the Po Valley. Their settlement proved fruitful and was often the cause of heated clashes over territory among the French, Spanish, and rivaling Italian duchies. The terrain's natural fertility continues to feed the nation's appetite for risotto, pasta, and polenta.

Nowhere will you find fresher pasta than in Milan. For a culinary experience that goes beyond the taste buds, follow your visit to the Dominican refectory (communal dining hall) of the Convent of Holy Mary of Grace (Santa Maria della Grazie) to see da Vinci's acclaimed Last Supper (*Cenacolo*) with your actual final meal of the day at traditional Milanese trattoria, Viaggi Nel Gusto!

The Northeast

Veneto

Veneto's Adriatic resorts complement the north's snow-capped Dolomites in winter or lush mountain trails in the summer. This region harbors age-old trade links with the East, kept alive over centuries by the solid commercial ambition of Venice, its capital. The unyielding glory of the Venetian empire, once facilitated by the Byzantines and other mighty powers, still grips the collective imagination of tourists and locals alike. Places there like St. Mark's Square (Piazza San Marco) and its nearby Basilica are a testament to the city's prestigious past.

After the ancient Venetians lost their taste for international trade once it became complicated by the waves of sieges during the

Crusades, they invested much of their wealth into surrounding land holdings.

With money pulsing through domestic networks around Veneto, the neighboring city of Verona flourished. These medieval dirt-trodden networks have now been converted into a car-laden tarmac—the expressway (*autostrada*)—which today links Venice to Verona, Padua, and Vicenza for modern-day travelers.

Emilia-Romagna

United by the Italian independence movement, Risorgimento, in the 19th century, the eastern Emilia region merged with Romagna to give us its current array of destinations. The thriving capital of Bologna is the site of the oldest university in Europe, erected in the 10th century on the foundations of a Roman law school dating back even further.

The bread-and-butter of Bologna serves up an incredible food culture that will leave you with a craving for "just one more helping." Dishing out a range of cured meats, fine cheeses, al dente pasta, and buttered pastries, this "breadbasket of Italy" is a must-see—and sample—for all foodies!

Friuli-Venezia Giulia

The peaceful beauty of Friuli-Venezia Giulia's geography, encompassing parts of the Dolomites as well as gulfs sloping from the Adriatic, mingles seamlessly with the region's vibrant history. Avid bookworms with a penchant for the classics will surely take a particular interest in the region's capital of Trieste, home to self-exiled writer James Joyce. In fact, Joyce's apartment above Picciòla's pharmacy on the Street of the Old Barrier (Via Della Barriera Vecchia) is still open to the public today.

Trentino-South Tyrol

The autonomous region of Trentino-South Tyrol is diverse, with over one million people inhabiting its picturesque mountain scenery. Around 55% have Italian as their mother tongue, while another 30%

speak a variation of German. The rest prefer one of the many languages spoken in the area's vibrant immigrant communities. Be sure to pinch yourself as you gaze upon the region's breathtaking landscapes, where sharp-headed peaks pierce blue skies that look stunning when reflected in the smooth waters of nearby lakes. Please take a moment to gaze upon all this breathtaking natural beauty surrounding you, capturing it in your memory for a lifetime.

The medieval center of Bolzano is a sleepy little city commonly enjoyed by hikers. In the capital's Museum of Archaeology, a Neolithic mummy named Ötzi the Iceman still gets his beauty sleep since his discovery on the Similaun Glacier in 1991.

Central Italy

Lazio

Imagine a spring in your step as you trace the hinterlands of Lazio just as many Romans likely did centuries before you as they marched to and from battle. Battered and exhausted, many high-class Roman generals took refuge in vacation homes by the sea or nearby lakes while waiting for the wounds of war to heal. Walk the old chariot roads to Tivoli on the edge of the Sabine hills. There, you'll find the haunting ruins of Emperor Hadrian's villa.

Central Italy is, without a doubt, the cradle of Roman civilization. The legacy of the ancient Empire is now best felt in the Eternal City, which still bears its name as the nation's capital. Naturally (*naturalmente*), Rome continues to be where the country's politics take center stage, from antiquity's Caesar to today's Meloni. Film lovers might like to pay tribute to Hepburn's classic role in *Roman Holiday* (1953) by climbing aboard a Vespa with a Peck look-alike of their own. Whizzing around Rome on one of these iconic vehicles offers a tour of the city like no other. The People's Square (Piazza del Popolo) and Trevi Fountain are also not to be missed!

Abruzzo

On the eastern flank of the center of the Italian peninsula lies Abruzzo, which yielded to Roman domination in the 3rd century BCE. Congratulate yourself if you dare to pull away from Rome's popularity for this delightful drift off the beaten track. The rugged wilderness of Abruzzo's National Park will reward you with fresh air, stunning vistas, and pleasant exercise. The walled regional capital of L'Aquila suffered greatly from the 2009 earthquake, but its beauty prevails nonetheless. Plus, the sandy coves of the Trabocchi Coast make for an excellent tonic should you need a cure for your lungs after days spent huffing and puffing around the Eternal City.

Marche

The patchwork fields of Marche weave their way between the Apennine Mountains and the Adriatic Sea. Ancona remains the region's central port city on the Conero Riviera (Riviera del Conero), with its attractive terracotta-tiled roofs and large windows–perfect for getting a few Mediterranean rays. From here, you might like to catch a ferry ride to Split in neighboring Croatia, where traces of the ancient Roman Empire survive to this day.

Tuscany

It was in Tuscany where the fusion of imagination and intellect, fantasy and science brought the Renaissance movement into the limelight. The delicate balance between light and dark can be seen clearly in Piero della Francesca's *Baptism of Christ* (1439), which illuminates the ways that such pioneers of that period immortalized their visions on the canvas. In 15th-century Florence, word was spreading in academic circles that the world might indeed be round–contrary to ecclesiastical teachings. Even more troubling for the Catholic Church, pamphlets were being printed to disseminate New World discoveries and all kinds of radical theories.

No stay will ever last long enough to cover all the sights of a big city, so during your visit to modern-day Florence, be extra mindful to favor quality over quantity. True, the Uffizi Gallery, Old Bridge (Ponte Vecchio), Cathedral Square (Piazza del Duomo), Baptistery of St. John (Battistero di San Giovanni), Medici-Riccardi Palace (Palazzo Medici-Riccardi), and Accademia Gallery are all spectacular in their own right. Still, if lounging around in a café people-watching is what you *really* want to do, please don't hesitate. Simply admiring the city and its people has just as much to offer as any Botticelli.

Tuscany's capital pulls millions into its orbit each year. First-timers may want to immerse themselves in the picture-taking crowds, but braving the 5-mile (8-km) climb (really, just 30 minutes by bus) to the nearby hill town of Fiesole will unveil yet another (and much calmer) version of this timeless treasure.

Umbria

Perhaps a bit overshadowed by the popularity of its Tuscan sister state, Umbria still shines in its own right. This blessedly less crowded region has much to offer with its culinary delights, spiritual significance, and dreamy landscape. Dominated by the papacy until Italian unification in 1861, Umbria continues to usher streams of students into the capital's Perugia University, founded by Pope Clement V in 1308.

Indulge in the city's sugar rush with a visit to the acclaimed Umbrian chocolate factory and museum, Perugina. This chocolaterie offers a slice of heaven for those with a sweet tooth and a passion for history. Top off your tour with a few signature *Baci* chocolates for dessert.

Southern Italy

Campania

The main pleasures of the south spring from the heart of its people; they are the gift to visitors that truly keeps on giving. Unclouded by the snobbishness that money often brings, the less prosperous southern regions–including Campania–remain rich in their music, food, and festivities. The delectable abundance offered by this region, grounded by its fertile volcanic soil, will make any hungry traveler's eyes pop out. Tomatoes, figs, olives, walnuts, oranges, and lemons are all locally grown and sold.

The menu only gets longer as you turn down the more obscure back-streets of Naples, the birthplace of pizza. There, pungent aromas of thick tomato sauce (*sugi di pomodoro*) and fresh sourdough waft through the air. Keep your valuables close as you peek through door-ways to catch a glimpse of Italy's legendary dish as it's being made. Don't tempt fate, or she will attempt a snatch-and-grab.

Campania's capital is neither the overly sentimental shtick of men bellowing to the chorus of 'O *Sole Mio* (1898), nor is it helplessly depressed and constantly subservient to the wealthier north. Instead, the reality of Naples rests somewhere in between.

Block your ears to the roar of traffic as you make your way down to Town Hall Square (Piazza Municipio). You'll appreciate an afternoon of boat-spotting by the docks.

Puglia

You'll find the Puglia region positioned at the "heel" of the peninsula. Puglia's white-washed hill townhouses (*trulli*) and 500 miles (805 km) of Mediterranean coastline make the region a great place to stop and rest as you ponder all the wonders you've encountered so far.

Massive fortresses and fortress-like churches like the Basilica of St. Nicholas (Basilica San Nicola) confirmed the safe passage of German emperors in days of old, not without leaving their own architectural marks, though!

Molise

This mountainous region stretches to engulf the coastline of the open Adriatic. Rich in wildlife, Molise is home to an ecosystem of fauna, some of which are regretfully in critical danger of becoming extinct. If you opt for a trail through the national park, be on the lookout for the fluffy Marsican brown bear, mighty wolf, and sprightly deer.

The regional capital, Campobasso, is famous for Monforte Castle (perched on the top of Mount Miletto (Monte Miletto)) and two churches featuring Romanesque architecture. To the north lies the Pietrabbondante archaeological area, where the cultural remnants of the Samnite people are still present.

Basilicata

Archaeology fanatics continue traveling in a trance as they pass through the densely forested area of Basilicata, which borders Puglia, Calabria, and the Ionian and Tyrrhenian Seas. You can visit ancient cave dwellings in the Sassi district, which is known for its complex geology and terrain at the surface level.

The capital, Potenza, enjoys its reputation as the highest regional capital in all of Italy. Don't overlook this stunning city!

Calabria

This "toe" of the peninsula is nothing to be ignored. Calabria is utterly sunbaked and steams intimations of romance, particularly under the unique natural structure of Arcomagno Beach (Spiaggia dell'Arcomagno). Under this phenomenal work of nature, broken hearts will be mended, and perhaps mending hearts will be broken anew. This is truly one of the dreamiest spots in Bella Italia.

Calabria's capital of Catanzaro, sometimes called the "City of the Two Seas," is vaguely reminiscent of nostalgic adventure stories like Sinbad (1885) and Treasure Island (1883). This is Italy's most narrow point, with only 18 miles (29 km) of land between the Tyrrhenian and Ionian coasts!

The Islands

Sicily

To truly do the island of Sicily any justice while sightseeing, if possible, a trip there should be planned as an entirely separate vacation. The vibrant hues of color you'll see at this quintessentially Mediterranean destination recall its Arab, Byzantine, and Norman inhabitants of days past.

The bustling capital of Palermo is a must-see. Lose yourself at the intersection of Vittoria Emanuele and Maqueda Streets (Via Vittoria Emanuele and Via Maqueda) in the city's center. There, you may feel yourself caught in the crossroads of history. Pulled by the Four Corners (Quattro Canti) of Palermo's old city, you will be pleased to fall into a calmer state when contemplating the 12th-century mosaics inside the Martorana Church's Arab-Norman haven.

Peering into the burning hell fires of Mount Etna's mouth is nothing short of Dante's dystopian *Inferno* (2003). I'm just joking; no guide in their right mind would ever ferry a tourist group up Sicily's iconically temperamental volcano if an eruption were likely. The route to Etna changes from year to year, lava permitting. If possible, try to organize an excursion to the crater, preferably timed to catch the sunset panorama!

Sardinia

As with Sicily, its smaller neighbor, Sardinia, the Mediterranean's second-largest island, is worth spoiling yourself with a second or third trip to Bella Italia. Need to cool off from all the head-spinning works of art created by the masters of antiquity and the Renaissance? Chilling out with your favored appetizer (*antipasto*) at a seaside Sardinian resort sounds like just the ticket!

Still, should the lifestyle of *il dolce far niente* (the sweetness of doing nothing) become too sickly-sweet, the island's capital, Cagliari, features a mix of influences sure to satisfy the cultural cravings of any history buff. The awe-inspiring wonders of the circular stone structures (*nuraghi*) are also not to be missed. Quaint and initially set down between 1900 and 730 BCE, these huts have seen countless transformations to their surrounding area, which was first colonized by the Phoenicians, then the Carthaginians, and later, the Romans. The nuraghi, however, have valiantly withstood the test of time.

WHAT TO DO BEYOND FAMOUS LANDMARKS

Off the beaten track, you'll discover an Italy no less fascinating than the one signed, sealed, and stamped on a postcard or tour pamphlet. Unearthing less-explored destinations there can put you in touch with a more authentic experience–if you know where to go!

Here are some ideas:

Explore Varenna at Lake Como

Favored by the most renowned Romantic poets, Wordsworth, Shelley, and Byron, wistful Lake Como has retained its age-old charm, welcoming visitors with its luxuriant array of surrounding greenery. The lake stretches out into two arms that come to rest on either side of the tranquil resort town of Bellagio. Gazing out onto the silky water, you'll see the coastal town of Varenna just a stone's skip away. With its medieval influences and quaint cobblestone streets, Varenna is a spot not to be missed if you need space and time to calm yourself from the busyness of the larger cities.

Hike the Dolomites

The majestic Dolomite Alps present a perfect balance of rich Alpine meadows and jagged white limestone flecked with rose-granite peaks. The Alps are often spoken of in the context of ski resorts and winter sports, but you'll find that the mountains in the eastern parts of the country have much to offer all year long. For brave-hearted and experienced trekkers, a hike up the Dolomites in the warmer seasons will provide incredible views and make lifelong memories.

Hike in Valsugana

Perhaps it's just the adrenaline, but as you descend the back of one Dolomite, you may keep up your stamina and continue your hike. The Sugana Valley, also known as Valsugana, is next up! Located just 74.5 miles (120 km) away from the Dolomites, these verdant fields in the province of Trentino offer some of the best scenery I have ever witnessed. What's more, if you find the right road, Claudia Augusta Way (Via Claudia Augusta), you'll be walking along the main north-south road from antiquity. This via winds along the valley to connect the Adriatic with what was once the glorious Holy Roman Empire and the central area of the then East Frankish kingdom, Augsburg.

Embark Upon the Barolo Wine Trail in Le Langhe

In the days before five-star reviews, Bishop Johannes Fugger of Augsburg sent out an advisor to visit the various inns, marking out which ones would be appropriate for the bishop's journey to Rome. The code word was *"est,"* which roughly translates to "this is it." This loyal gentleman stumbled upon an especially tasty treasure in one of the local inns and could not contain his exclamations of *"Est, est, est!"* Upon arriving, the bishop is said to have drunk himself so silly that he went all the way to his grave. The tomb itself is located in the Church of San Flaviano, with this merry Latin inscription testifying to his delicious cause of death — wine — which in Bella Italia is clearly revered as one of humankind's most faithful companions. All jokes aside, the UNESCO-protected hills of Le Langhe in the north will definitely leave you thinking, "This *is* it!"

Barolo's wine trail along the valley promises to tantalize the senses, from the landscape's spectacular visuals to the tastings at 10th-century Castle Barolo itself. Sipping a glass of this glorious red under the sun here is the perfect way to finish off an active afternoon.

Taste Limoncello Like No Other in Sorrento

From the sirens that tempted Ulysses and his crew in vain to today's street guitarists, Sorrento has lost none of its famous enchantment, and for good reason. The sinuous coast curving along the southern arm of the Bay of Naples will lull anyone into a romantic trance—even the most audacious of drivers!

As you continue to ease into Sorrento's gentle rhythms, a glass of limoncello will guarantee you an authentic Campania experience. The region is abundant with citrus goodies, so it would be cruel to neglect a tasting of this signature lemon liqueur (only if you're a drinker, of course!).

Wander the Streets of Siracusa

Palermo is a given destination when many plan their travels to Sicily. Heard less often are the raves of those fortunate enough to stroll the friendly, sun-drenched streets of Siracusa near the island's eastern coast. Passed from Greek to Roman hands, this city was the birthplace of pioneer mathematician Archimedes, the genius who had his legendary "eureka" moment upon understanding the principles of buoyancy and displacement of water while sitting in his bathtub.

Beyond its intellectual history, Siracusa's adjoining island, Ortigia, has its own particular charm, which is not to be missed. Be sure to check out the ancient open-air Necropolis, and then follow it up with an espresso at the renowned Café Letterario near the Temple of Apollo.

Wintering in Cinque Terre

While the water may be too cold for a swim (unless ice baths are your thing), escaping the crowds with a winter visit to Cinque Terre on the Italian Riviera is a smart move. The peace of the surrounding fishing villages and comfortable daytime highs of 68°F (20°C) are sure to chase away any winter blues.

LOCAL FAVORITES BEYOND TOURIST HOTSPOTS

According to a local, "In Italy, there's something for every taste. Everywhere and anywhere is a holiday destination for someone."

Come August, the country slowly comes to a stop. Vendors pack away their wares in the smoldering 104°F (40°C) heat while parents prepare themselves for school to begin again for their children.

What would *you* do if you already lived in one of the world's most celebrated holiday destinations?

Over a few friendly dinners and between some of the work shifts I've shared with Tuscans, Sicilians, and Milanese, I have managed to gather some hidden gems only known to and experienced by locals during vacation—until now!

Tuscia, Lazio

Every year, without fail, the summer heat, mingled with being in a hurry to fill the gas tank, drives the Romans out of the Eternal City for the weekend and into the vineyards of the Alban Hills and lakes. A cool glass of wine will refresh you along the way to the ancient city of Tuscia as you make stopovers in the nearby country villages of Frascati and Marino. Be sure to stay the night and not drive light-headed from all the region's charm!

Urbino, Marche

Straddling the hills in the central Marche region, the municipality (*comune*) of Urbino was the birthplace of one of Italy's greatest Renaissance painters, Raffaello. The galleries here contain works by this native son as well as Piero della Francesca and Titian. Urbino is also a lively university town teeming with students, some of whom you'll find tearing off a piece of *crescia* (a lard-moistened flatbread filled with anything from chard to ham and cheese) as they let off some steam on the Park of the Resistance (Parco della Resistenza), a green space below medieval ruins.

Monte Argentario, Tuscany

In our pursuit of doing as the Romans, we come to rest in Tuscany's southern stretch of pine-forested coast, which brushes borders with Lazio.

Here, you'll find the beaches of Monte Argentario, a promontory bound to the mainland by two thick sandbars. While many locals flock to Argentario for the weekend, I'd advise you to travel there during the week to avoid the crowds.

Alpe di Siusi, South Tyrol

Beach or mountain? It's a tough decision. Up in the Dolomites lies Alpe di Siusi, a landscape of rolling meadows. The modern chalet-style hotel, Adler Lodge Alpe, offers stunning peak views that are almost always accompanied by the light jingle of cowbells from an Alpine hut where cheese is produced (*malga*) nestled just a few minutes' walk away.

Salento, Puglia

At the very "heel" of Italy, you'll find yourself on Salento's sleepy peninsula. Its unspoiled beauty resides in the main city of Lecce, filled with Roman ruins and Baroque architecture.

Camogli, Liguria

Ever the understated Riviera town, Camogli fills the Ligurian coast with color. Its candy-colored houses hem the pebbly bay, which has not (yet) been thwarted by tourists. Here, it's the locals of yesteryear, the year before, and the year before, too! The town feels like it was designed especially for wanderers, so climb up to the 13th-century fortification of Dragone Castle (Castello della Dragonara) for views overlooking the sea.

Zip down by car to the San Fruttuoso Bay, and you'll discover *Christ of the Abyss*, an underwater statue of Jesus throwing his arms from the seabed. With all its spiritual and culinary connotations, this body of water is an integral part of the area's cultural identity. Fish lovers won't want to miss the annual fish festival of Sagra del Pesce in May, where the townspeople prepare a huge fry-up of the day's catch in an enormous pan by the sea.

Trieste, Friuli Venezia Giulia

Trieste's Italian Unity Square (Piazza Unità d'Italia) is the largest public square in Europe that faces the water. Central beaches like Lanterna and Ausonia are very popular. When the monotony of daily life becomes too much, Venetian residents retreat just 90 minutes away to this city. Adopting Italian nationality only recently in 1920, Trieste used to be in the Austro-Hungarian Empire. Traces of its history are visible in the Grand Habsburg-era buildings that face the piazza. Typical Austrian strudel and *Sachertorte* can be acquired at little cubby hole cafés, all of which show off the city's diverse history.

Capo Vaticano, Calabria

International visitors don't tend to visit the uneven Calabrian "toe" of the country very much. Instead, the Italians themselves shower the care and attention on Capo Vaticano that its Amalfi-style towns, coastal roads, and vibrant views of the water rightly deserve. The sandy coves and beaches surrounding Capo Vaticano also draw in summer visitors from throughout the country. All of this is set against the dramatic backdrop of the Stromboli Volcano (which lies on an island of the same name). Any visit to Capo Vaticano would be incomplete without a taste of the local delicacy, *tartufo*–a heavenly chocolate and hazelnut gelato dessert filled with molten chocolate sauce.

Pantelleria

Clear days on this oval-shaped island will reveal closer views of Tunisia than the Bel Paese. Wedged between two mainlands, this speck of coast is the place to disconnect, with the terrible phone signal helping you do just that. Traditional white-domed *dammusi* houses lie on the sloping hills with little to do here but to join you in sitting back, resting, and gazing out onto the crystal-clear waters. The sulfur-rich thermal waters of Mirror of Venus Lake (Lago Specchio di Venere) in an old volcanic crater make for an unforgettable natural outdoor spa day.

Macerata, Marche

While foreigners rush to Tuscany, residents love neighboring Marche, or so common knowledge goes. While the natural background is more or less the same on the other side of the Apennine Mountains from Tuscany and Umbria, there are fewer visitors here. Plan to dedicate at least a full day here. It'll definitely take you that long to tour the local art gallery—Buonaccorsi Palace (Palazzo Buonaccorsi)—as well as the smaller hilltop towns nearby.

POCKETS OF PEACE

Tellaro, Liguria

On the edge of the Gulf of Poets (Golfo dei Poeti), it was in the area of Tellaro where 18th-century Romantics like Shelley and Byron found inspiration. Today, writers and artists continue to let the town's tranquility and natural beauty infuse their work. This spot is a pure coastal paradise and remains one of the country's best-kept secrets.

Pitigliano, Tuscany

Just one hour inland from Maremma lies Pitigliano. Perched at the top of the canyon's edge, this town has long been nicknamed Italy's "Little Jerusalem" for its 15th-century Jewish heritage. While most of Pitigliano's Jews moved to other towns by the late 1930s, you can still visit the old ghetto. There, you'll find the restored synagogue (Tempio Israelitico di Pitigliano), which is part of the the town's Jewish Museum.

Procida, Campania

As with books and their covers, never judge a destination by its size. Procida is a tiny isle in the Bay of Naples (with an area of 1.4 square miles or 3.6 square kilometers), and visitors often bypass it as they make a beeline to see nearby Capri and Ischia. Yet, with a rainbow of colored buildings overlooking its picture-perfect harbor, this treasure of an island looks like something taken straight from a movie set. Its highest and oldest point, Terra Murata, is definitely worth the climb.

Chioggia, Veneto

If you imagine what Venice could have looked like 2,000 years ago, it might look a little something like Chioggia. Accessible by bus and ferry from Venice, Chioggia's layout also incorporates waterways, similar to the Floating City but without the crowds. If you can, arrive in the morning to get a whiff of the traditional fish market and follow this up with a seaside lunch along the Adriatic.

Locorotondo, Puglia

This part of Puglia is home to several white-hill towns, and Locorotondo is the one I'd recommend. The city, famous for its white wine, is best experienced while overlooking the dramatic skyline, which is dominated by the Mother Church of St. George (Chiesa Madre San Giorgio).

Viterbo, Lazio

Venture just two hours from Rome by train, and you'll end up in the beautiful city of Viterbo. This medieval marvel was once the 13th-century papal seat, which can still be admired in the historic Pope's Palace (Palazzo dei Papi) in St. Lawrence Square (Piazza San Lorenzo). Spare a couple of hours and try Viterbo's thermal baths, a treat that has been savored by locals and visitors alike for centuries.

Noto, Sicily

Noto, a town once leveled by an earthquake in 1693, is now the beautiful slanted city we know today. Its Baroque churches and elegant palaces were constructed only after the fatal tremors, giving the area a seeming sense of balance.

Saluzzo, Piedmont

Admired by few yet valued by all who've visited, this rare Italian destination offers the chance to discover cultural treasures. Visit the sloping edifice of Casa Cavassa, with its arched Renaissance-era ceilings, intricate frescoes, and antique furniture. Stroll at your leisure through the flourishing botanical garden at Villa Bricherasio.

Spello, Umbria

One of Umbria's less-traveled villages, Spello is just a 15-minute drive from Assisi. Nonetheless, the hustle and bustle feels worlds away as you breeze through the city's Roman walls and quiet churches—with little to no wait time.

If you happen to be in Spello at the beginning of June, bask in the vibrant Infiorate festival to commemorate the warming of the season. You'll marvel at the murals made of flower petals blooming throughout the streets and squares as the locals reveal their authentic community spirit.

Bosa, Sardinia

The charming "flags" of Italy's ubiquitous hanging laundry are draped over the streets of Bosa in western Sardinia. This riverfront town is distinguished by the mismatch of hillside houses washed in every color under the sun while the Castle of Serravalle looms above. Seafood with an appetizer (*antipasto*) on a terrace with a view is one of Bosa's essentials!

Chiusa/Klausen, Trentino-South Tyrol

The Isarco River northeast of Venice forms the basin of Chiusa (also known as Klausen), which offers stunning scenic views, charming shops, winding cobblestone lanes, and friendly locals. Be sure to spare a few hours to make the climb uphill to the area around the Benedictine Sabiona Monastery, established in 1699. While the monastery itself isn't open to the public, you'll be able to visit the nearby Liebfrauenkirche church.

COASTAL RETREATS AND SECLUDED BEACHES

Riomaggiore Beach, Cinque Terre

At Riomaggiore, you'll have dramatic cliffs behind you as you enjoy swimming in its clear blue waters. You can rent a beach chair and umbrella from one of the private clubs. If you get there early, you can also claim a spot in the beach's small free area!

Bidderosa Beach, Sardinia

The secluded, silver-sand beach of Bidderosa, located near the town of Orosei, is part of a nature reserve where daily admission is limited. Once you've purchased a ticket at the Forest Station of Orosei, you can make your way down the 2.4-mile (3.9-km) path, fragrant with the scent of juniper and pine, to the beach below.

Bagni della Regina Giovanna, Campania

Located near Sorrento, the spectacular cove of the Baths of Queen Giovanna (Bagni della Regina Giovanna) is hidden. The rocky slopes surrounding it may be a bit tricky to manage at first, but the luminous waters and stony archway linking this lagoon to the sea make it well worth the effort. You can also reach the lagoon by boat.

Laurito, Amalfi Coast

Laurito is only one of the Amalfi Coast's best-kept secrets. Although it's popular with the locals, this hidden gem is at no risk of being overrun by tourists. Stretch out and watch as the waves lap the dark sand and pebbles. To get there, you can take a bus above the path climbing down to Laurito or a shuttle boat that leaves from Positano's main jetty.

Cala Luna, Sardinia

The crescent-shaped beach of Cala Luna is nestled on Sardinia's northwestern coast near Dorgali. Its clear, shallow waters make Cala Luna an ideal option for families traveling with small children.

Adventurers will marvel at the six small caves nearby as well as the Del Bue Marino grotto, which can only be accessed by boat. To get to Cala Luna, you can hike in from Cali Fuili or Balnei or go by boat. If you are traveling with small children, I recommend the latter option, which is from the Cala Gonone port or Marina di Orosei.

Dino Island, Praia a Mare, Calabria

The jagged outcrop called Dino Island sits just 328 feet (100 meters) from Praia a Mare. There, you'll find coves and sea caves you can paddle into by raft. Scuba diving is also very popular. Get an adrenaline high by taking the 67-foot (20.4-meter) cliff jump off Arcomagno Rock, Praia a Mare's natural bridge structure.

Tordigliano Beach, Amalfi Coast

Another of the Amalfi Coast's jewels is Tordigliano Beach, located 9 miles (14 km) from Sorrento. The three pebbled beaches all offer lovely views of the Li Galli islands. Most visitors come by boat, but it is also possible to reach Tordigliano by taking a rough 1.2-mile (1.9-km) trail beginning at SS Road Amalfitana no. 163.

Cala Mariolu, Sardinia

The lapis lazuli waters and rosy pebbles of Cala Mariolu Beach work their magic on all who visit. The calm, shallow water allows families with young children to enjoy the day out together and maybe even go snorkeling! The trek to Cala Mariolu can be a bit arduous, so I'd recommend going there by boat from Cala Gonone, Arbatax, or Santa Maria Navarrese.

Riserva Dello Zingaro, Sicily

Sicily's white-sand Riserva Dello Zingaro Beach sits undisturbed in the protected area of the island, offering a perfect place to relax.

Macarro Beach, Basilicata

Macarro Beach is a small, local favorite featuring black sand and a scenic overlook of the sparkling Tyrrhenian Sea. To get there, take a short hike down a steep path from the nearby parking lot.

Santa Croce Beach, Amalfi Coast

The beauty of this spot draws crowds during peak season in July and August, but for the rest of the year, you won't be disturbed. Get there by boat or by walking down the stairs from the Amalfi Coast Road, where you can savor your lunch at one of the local restaurants.

MOUNTAIN ESCAPES

Courmayeur

The quaint town of Courmayeur sits near the French border in one of the smallest regions of Italy. The surrounding valleys offer beautiful hiking, skiing, and snowboarding paths. Mont Blanc stands here just as majestically as ever—the tallest in the Alps! Dangle from the Skyway cable car over this massive mountain for the full panoramic experience.

Livigno

Livigno is Bella Italia's best hidden gem. The Alpine town lies just 120 miles (193 km) north of Milan and is popular among mountain bikers, hikers, and skiers. Livigno feels like it was made especially for the adventurous. Be sure to make the one-hour drive to the glacier at the Stelvio Pass, the only one in the nation that can be skied or snowboarded year-round.

After a long day of winter sports, sitting down to a dinner of Livigno's local pasta (pizzoccheri) and polenta taragna will be well worth the effort. For cocktail lovers, this region's own hot Bombardino eggnog will also go down as a treat!

Montepulciano

Close to Val d'Orcia in the province of Siena, Montepulciano is most famous for its red wine. Get your hands on a glass by diving into the little cantinas throughout the city, many of which offer complimentary tastings.

Bagni San Filippo

The calcium-enriched thermal baths of San Filippo are situated in the sparser area of Val d'Orcia. With little to no entertainment in this tiny town other than these natural pools, you can take a break from travel planning and enjoy the peaceful moments to be found there.

Castelluccio di Norcia

A backdrop of jagged mountains and open sky frames the stunning views of Castelluccio di Norcia. As part of the Monti Sibillini National Park, this town brushes both the Umbrian and Marche borders.

ANDIAMO (LET'S GO)...

The Bel Paese *is* the gift that keeps on giving. One region will lead you on to the next in high spirits. From the snowy north all the way down to the balmy south, there truly is a place to suit every traveler's taste. So far, I've introduced you to each region and its capital. The big cities have been covered as much as towns that are only marked by the crease of a map. I hope you've found something within this specially crafted list of destinations that piques your interest. Be careful, though, as you may discover a new favorite along the way!

Wherever your Italian travels take you, you'll want to engage with the locals, whether it's to ask for help or express your gratitude. The next chapter will walk–and talk–you through the basics of local lingo.

MAKE A DIFFERENCE WITH YOUR REVIEW
UNLOCK THE POWER OF GENEROSITY

"Helping others is the way we help ourselves."

OPRAH WINFREY

People who give without expecting anything in return live happier, longer lives. They even find more success. So, during our time together, let's make a big difference.

Would you help someone you've never met, even if you never got credit for it?

Who is this person? They're just like you. Or like you used to be. They're less experienced, wanting to make a difference, needing help, but not sure where to look.

My mission is to make travel to Italy accessible to everyone. Everything I do is to support that mission. And, the only way for me to achieve it is by reaching...well...everyone.

This is where you come in. Most people judge a book by its cover (and its reviews). So, here's my ask on behalf of a struggling person about to travel to Italy, whether they're a solo adventurer, LGBTQIA+ traveler, woman, family, or couple you've never met:

Please help that person by leaving a review for this book.

Your gift costs no money and takes less than 60 seconds, but it can change a fellow traveler's life forever. Your review could help...

...one more mother feel safe taking her children to Rome...one more young man find himself and discover his passions in Florence...one more Queer person feel acceptance and a sense of community in Milan...one more family reconnect and create lifelong memories in

Lake Garda...one more couple go on their once-in-a-lifetime vacation to Sicily...one more Italian dream come true.

To get that "feel good" feeling and help this person, all you have to do is...leave a review.

Simply scan the QR code below:

If you feel good about helping a faceless struggling person about to travel to Italy, you're my kind of person. Welcome to the group. You're one of us.

I'm that much more excited to help you travel safer, discover hidden Italian gems, learn the lingo, and experience authentic Italian culture faster than you can imagine. You'll love what I'm about to share in the coming chapters.

Thank you from the bottom of my heart.

    - Your biggest fan, Maria Tuminelli

PS - If you provide something of value to another person, it makes you more valuable to them. If you believe this book will help someone, please send it their way.

CHAPTER 4
A CRASH COURSE IN LOCAL LINGO

> *Nowhere is civilization so perfectly mirrored as in speech. If our knowledge of speech, or the speech itself, is not yet perfect, neither is civilization.*

MARIO PEI, *THE STORY OF LANGUAGE* (1965)

THE ITALIAN LANGUAGE

As the expression of human activity, the communication tool we call "language" changes just as often as humans are changed by it.

The Latin tongue, the predecessor of modern Italian and the other Romance languages, remains one of the world's oldest. We have a complete, unbroken record of it from 500 BCE to the end of the Roman Empire and beyond.

When Latin first appeared around the mouth of the Tiber River in Central Italy, it was the tongue of a small group of settlers who originated from what is now Northern Europe. The history of these Latin speakers and their language was a bitter struggle for survival, particularly against the Etruscans. By the middle of the 3rd century BCE,

Rome had established its dominance over the Italian mainland, subjugating the Etruscans and pushing the Gauls back to the foothills of the Alps. Rome and her elemental spoken word were ready to embark on a journey of transformation. However, the classical refinements of syntax and vocabulary of early Rome had not yet emerged, as Rome was chiefly committed to military conquests.

The smoother, polished version used by Caesar, Cicero, and Virgil emerged during Latin's Golden Era in 100 BCE, when the language found its way into poetry, oratory, and politics.

The "Big Three" Tuscan poets of the 14th century–Dante Alighieri, Giovanni Boccaccio, and Francesco Petrarch–fell into a similar artistic step. The fortunate accident of their presence and preeminence in Italian literature has led many to this day to make the exaggerated assertion that "Italian" is synonymous with "Tuscan."

Little attention is paid to the various dialects, which are still widely used, even by the younger generations. Because today's Italy was once a complex assembly of individual duchies before its unification in 1861, the persistence of these vernaculars is not so surprising.

The cultural richness flowing from these modes of interaction reflects Italy's diverse national identity. The stereotype that dialects such as Sicilian, Neapolitan, and Sardinian are "vulgar spins" of the Florentine tongue is simply incorrect. Although the "standard" Italian taught in schools was originally spoken in Central Tuscany, the people are proud of the dozens of other local dialects they keep alive and well. In fact, recent statistics reveal, for example, that in one of the most economically developed regions, Veneto, around half of the people speak in dialect both with their families and friends (I.Stat, 2024).

Taking in the brilliant squares (*piazze*) of Veneto in Venice, Padua, Treviso, Verona, or Vicenza, you'll soon hear just how present a dialect can be. While no one is expecting you to unveil a perfect Venetian dialect on your first trip (or even standard Italian, for that matter), having some degree of awareness is the politest way to travel.

Plus, learning even the most basic pleasantries will help you make authentic connections with the locals you'll later remember fondly as an integral part of your Italian adventure.

ESSENTIAL ITALIAN PHRASES FOR SEAMLESS TRAVEL

Market Interactions

You and your family of early birds are passing through the Rialto market as the sun begins to peek out from behind the morning clouds in the "Floating City" of Venice. As you make your way through the aisles, baskets overflow with tomatoes (*pomodori*) giving off a scent too delectable to resist. They're nothing like the plastic-encased ones you know all too well back in the markets at home. You decide then and there to buy at least one pound (0.45 kg) of these juicy ruby-colored jewels. How do you go about this?

Common Greetings:

You'll see the English translation, the Italian word(s), and finally, the Italian pronunciation!

- Good morning (formal) / *Buongiorno* / *Bwohn-JOHR-noh*
- Good afternoon / *Buon pomeriggio* / *Bwohn poh-meh-REED-joh*
- Good evening (formal) / *Buonasera* / *Bwoh-nah-SEH-rah*
- Hi or Bye (informal) / *Ciao!* / *Cheeow*
- Good night (formal) / *Buona notte* / *Bwoh–nah–NOH–teh*
- How are you? (formal) / *Come sta?* / *Koh-meh stah?*
- Good, thank you / *Bene, grazie* / *BEH-neh, GRAH-tsee-eh*
- Goodbye (formal) / *Arrivederci* / *Ahr-ree-veh-DEHR-chee*

Other Useful Phrases:

- Excuse me (for attention) / *Scusi* / *SKOO–zee*
- Do you speak English? / *Parla Inglese?* / *PAHR-la een-GLAY-zeh*

- I don't understand / *Non capisco* / *Non-kah-PEE-skoh*
- So, then / *Allora* / *ah - LLOR - ah*
- I'd like ... / *Vorrei ...* / *V - oh – RRAYE ...*
- Please / *Per favore* / *Pehr fah-VOH-reh*
- Thank you (Thanks a lot) / *Grazie (Grazie mille)* / *GRAH-tsee-eh (MEE - leh)*

Numbers:

- One / *Uno* / *OO-noh*
- Two / *Due* / *DOO-eh*
- Three / *Tre* / *Treh*
- Four / *Quattro* / *KWAH-troh*
- Five / *Cinque* / *CHEEN-kweh*
- Six / *Sei* / *Say*
- Seven / *Sette* / *SEHT-tey*
- Eight / *Otto* / *OH-toh*
- Nine / *Nove* / *NOH-veh*
- Ten / *Dieci* / *Dee-EH-chee*
- Eleven / *Undici* / *OON–dee-chee*
- Twelve / *Dodici* / *DOH-dee-chee*

Finally, Yes and No:

- Yes / *Si* / *See*
- No / *No* / *Noh*

Navigation

One pound (0.45 kg) of pomodori heavier, you're all set. The streets of Venice are yawning through a slow and sleepy start to this Saturday morning. Nonetheless, you realize that they are beginning to narrow and that you need to make room for oncoming traffic.

To Pass by Politely:

- I'm sorry / *Mi dispiace* / *Mee dees-PYAH-cheh*
- Excuse me / *Permesso* / *Pehr-MEHS-soh*
- You're welcome / *Prego* / *PREH-goh*

Was it at Calle dei Morti or Campo Santa Margherita where you were supposed to take a right turn? Squeezing yourself flat to pass through the bustling noontime of Venice has made you lose your bearings. The blessed "I" sign at the end of the road sticks out to become your saving grace. You make your way to the tourist information desk to ask for directions.

To Ask for Directions (always following the usual formalities of "hello" and "how are you?"):

- Where is…? / *Dov'è…?* / *Doh-VEH …* ?
- Where is the bus stop? / *Dov'è la fermata?* / *Doh-VEH lah fair-MAH-tah?*
- Where is the train station? / *Dov'è la stazione?* / *Doh-VEH lah stah-tzee-OH-neh?*
- Back / *Dietro* / *Dee-ATE-roh*
- Forward / *Avanti* / *Ah-VAHN-tee*
- Straight ahead / *Dritto* / *DREE-toh*
- Left / *Sinistra* / *See–NEE-stra*
- Right / *Destra* / *DEH-stra*
- Exit / *Uscita* / *OOH-shee-tah*
- Entrance / *Entrata* / *En-TRAH-tah*

The friendly tourist agent has set you back on the right course. After a quick stop for a snack of fresh tomato sandwiches, you're off to catch the afternoon train to Padua, where you hope to spend the rest of the day. Now, with your new knowledge of directions, it's easy to reach the train station; you almost feel like a local.

You planned, but in the rush of travel preparations, you forgot to buy your tickets in advance. No matter—you and your family head to the station's ticket desk to make the purchase.

For Transportation Questions:

- One (or) two tickets / *Un biglietto (o) Due biglietti* / *Oon beel-YEH-toh (oh) DOO-eh beel-YEH-tee*
- One way / *Andata* / *Ahn–DAH-tah*
- Return / *Ritorno* / *Ree-TORN-oh*
- What platform for ...? / *Da quale binario per ... ?* / *Dah kwah-lay bee-NAH-ree-oh pehr ... ?*
- *Newsstand (for bus tickets)* / *Tabacchi* / *Tah-BAHK-kee*

The rolling hills drape over the verdant fields of Veneto as you gaze out the window of your high-speed train bound for Padua. Everyone boarded fine with the help of the kind porter back at the Mestre station. You rest your eyes briefly, calm in the knowledge that your Italian adventure will resume in a half hour!

Phrases for Visiting Museums and Attractions

Padua, or so you've read, features one of the most captivating frescos in all of Italy. In the interior of the Arena Chapel (Cappella degli Scrovegni), Giotto's intricate masterpiece remains intact. You cannot wait to share your excitement for the vaulted paintings with your family as you make a beeline for the chapel, smartphone GPS app in hand.

When you arrive at the kiosk, you wish to buy entry tickets to see these famed frescos.

When Visiting Museums and Other Local Attractions:

- When does it open (or) close? / *Quando si apri (o) chiude?* / *KWAHN-doh see AH-pree (oh) kee-OO-deh?*

- One (or) two ticket(s) / *Un (o) due biglietto(i)* / *Oon beel-YET-toh (oh) DOO-eh beel-YET-tee*
- Two adults (or) one child / *Due adulti (o) un bambino* / *DOO-eh ah-DOOL-tee (oh) oon bahm-BEE-noh*
- One student / *Uno studente* / *OOH-noh stoo-DEN-teh*
- One senior / *Un pensionato* / *Oon pen-see-yoh-NAH-toh*
- Where is the bag store (*cloak room*)? / *Dov'è la guardaroba?* / *Doh-VEH lah gward-ah-ROBE-ah?*

The frescos were incredible. As you emerge from the chapel into the fresh, open air, your stupor fades a little when you notice that your partner (not at all an art lover) is already looking up the next thing to do. They compromised on attending Giotto's art, so now it's your turn to let them take the reins.

Shopping Words in Italian

One word: shopping. Maybe it's not your thing, but it's undoubtedly the kids' and your partner's. Since your first bite of breakfast at St. Mark's Square (Piazza San Marco), your partner has fallen head over heels in love with authentic Italian coffee. Now, they won't settle for less than a freshly ground and brewed cup of arabica beans. It might sound snobbish to you, but they simply *must* go home with a compact version of the renowned Bialetti French press (*cafetière*).

Your phone's map takes you right up to the doorstep of the homeware shop. The prices for these percolators are astoundingly high. You glance at your partner, trying to make eyes with them to abort their mission, but it's futile. They are determined to walk away with a (relatively useful) Italian souvenir.

When Making a Purchase:

- I would like… / *Vorrei…* / *Vor-RAY…*
- How much is this? / *Quanto costa questo?* / *Kwahn-toh KOHS-tah KWEHS-toh?*

- I don't want it / *Non lo voglio* / *Nohn loh VOH-lyoh*
- OK, I'll take it / *Va bene, lo prendo* / *Vah BEH-neh, loh PREHN-doh*
- Can you ship to...? / *Puoi spedire a?* / *Pwoy spayd-EAR-eh ah?*

A cafetière design chosen, neither you nor your partner are prepared to make the payment, even after you tried haggling. You suggest to your family that it may be best to think about it and return later if and when you and your partner make the final decision. You'd like to know what this shop's hours are.

Asking for the Time and Days of the Week:

- In the morning / *Di mattina* / *Dee mah-TEEN-ah*
- In the afternoon / *Di pomeriggio* / *Dee poh-meh-REED-joh*
- In the evening / *Di sera* / *Dee SEH–rah*
- Noon / *Mezzogiorno* / *Mehd-dzoh-JOHR-noh*
- At what time? / *A che ora?* / *Ah kay OAR-ah?*
- Nine o'clock in the morning / *Le nove* / *Leh NOH-vay*
- Eight o'clock in the evening / *Le otto di sera* / *Leh OT-to dee SEH-rah*
- Monday / *Lunedì* / *Loo-neh-DEE*
- Tuesday / *Martedì* / *Mahr-teh-DEE*
- Wednesday / *Mercoledì* / *Mehr-koh-leh-DEE*
- Thursday / *Giovedì* / *Joh-veh-DEE*
- Friday / *Venerdì* / *Veh-nehr-DEE*
- Saturday / *Sabato* / *SAH-bah-toh*
- Sunday / *Domenica* / *Doh-MEH-nee-kah*
- Today / *Oggi* / *OHD-jee*
- Yesterday / *Ieri* / *YEH-ree*
- Tomorrow / *Domani* / *Doh-MAH-nee*

Indulging in Restaurants and Cafés

The sun's rays slowly disintegrate behind the steeple of St. Anthony's Basilica (Basilica di Sant'Antonio), leaving a wash of pinks and pallid blues in their midst. You take a deep breath, satisfied with a day that began with the toll of church bells and will surely end with similarly sweet music. In the terraced restaurant, you lean back in your seat and dip in and out of the conversation unfolding around the table as your family waits to order dinner. You feel a smile tugging at the corners of your mouth as you become vaguely aware of your partner closely inspecting their prized Bialetti coffee maker. In the end, something had to give!

Everything is just as it should be, and the thought of a delicious meal inspires you to give the waiter a small wave. You are perfectly calm as he eases between the sea of occupied chairs and tables. You have zero qualms about ordering in Italian, not after the time you've spent learning these useful phrases:

- May I see the menu, please? / *Il menu, per favore* / *Eel mehn-OO, pehr fah-VOH-reh*
- What do you recommend? / *Che cosa ci consiglia?* / *Kay KOH-za chee kohn-SEEL-ya?*
- I'm allergic to... / *Sono allergica(o) a...* / *Sohn-oh ah-LER-jee-koh / kah ah*
- Gluten, Dairy, Fish / *Glutine, Lattecini, Pesce* / *Gloo-TEEN-ay, Lah-tay-CHEEN-ee, PESH-ay*
- House wine / *Vino della casa* / *Vee-noh del-lah CAH-sah*
- Red (or) White wine / *Vino rosso (o) bianco* / *Vee–noh RO-soh (oh) bee-AHN-koh*
- A glass (or) bottle / *Una bicchiere (o) una bottiglia* / *Oo-nah beek-YEH-reh (oh) oo-nah boht-TEE-lyah*
- Appetizer / *Antipasto* / *Ahn-tee-PAH-stoh*
- First course / *Primo* / *PREE-moh*
- Second course / *Secondo* / *Say-KOHN-doh*

- Dessert / *Dolci* / *DOAL-chee*
- Two flavors please / *Due gusti, per favore* / *Doo-eh GOO-stee, pehr fah-VOH-reh*
- The check (bill) please / *Il conto, per favore* / *Eel KON-toh, pehr fah-VOH-reh*
- Where's the restroom? / *Dov'è il bagno?* / *Doh-VEH eel BAHN-yoh?*
- May I pay by card? / *Posso pagare con la carta?* / *Pohs-soh pah-GAH-reh kon la CAHR-tah?*
- Cheers! (To your health) / *Salute!* / *Sah-LOO-teh*

Meeting People

The real difficulty on your trip will be *not* running into friendly conversations with Italians. When you find yourself in this likely situation, be prepared with these introductions:

- What is your name? / *Come si chiama?* / *Koh-meh see KYAH-mah?*
- My name is ... / *Mi chiamo* / *Mee KYAH-moh*
- Do you speak English? / *Parla inglese?* / *Parlah Een-GLAY-zeh?*
- Pleased to meet you / *Piacere* / *Pyah-CHEH-reh*

Emergency and Safety Phrases

I hope you'll never need to use these emergency phrases, but it's a good idea to have them ready just in case. (*See emergency contact details and more information on safety in Chapter 2*)

Emergency Phrases:

- Help! / *Aiuto!* / *Ay-OO-toh!*
- Call the police / *Chiami la polizia* / *Kee-YA-mee la poh-lee-TSEE-ah*

- I need a doctor / *Ho bisogno di un dottore* / *Oh beez-OHN-nyo dee oon doh-TOR-reh*
- Go away! / *Vai via!* / *Vye VEE-ah!*
- Look out! / *Attento!* / *Ah–TEN-toh!*

SOUNDING IT OUT...

Now that you're equipped with the right foundations for speaking Italian, you're all set to start making cultural connections–of which there are so many! On occasion, Italians will take music out of the concert halls to fill their streets with Vivaldi, Puccini, and Verdi. Life is at its climax during these festivities, and soon, you will be able to join in this glorious cacophony. From music and celebrations to intimate and formal interactions over a hearty meal, the next chapter will lead you through the bounty of delights that pervade Italian culture.

CHAPTER 5

ITALY'S CULTURAL WONDERS

Italy is full of actors, almost all fifty million of them good, while the few bad ones actually made it to the stage or the silver screen.

ORSON WELLES (ANILE, 2013)

The vibrancy of the country's people, customs, and culture will convince just about any visitor that they've found their "home away from home." Like with any good performance, though, there is a loose script to follow–at least for a basic understanding of how best to join in on the fun.

This chapter will teach you about Italian etiquette, festivities, eating out, and artistic heritage to ensure you will not be embarrassed when you're at the dinner table or out among the locals.

NAVIGATING CULTURAL ETIQUETTE AND CUSTOMS

One of the liveliest spectator sports practiced by Italians and watched by crowds of bemused foreigners is the people's art of communication–mainly through gestures. To show kindness and respect to the locals, I recommend that you also use this body language when inter-acting. Remember — first impressions are lasting, and they'll likely feel more comfortable around you when they see you moving like them.

Ignoring a few commuters soured by urban stress, most Italians are as warm and outgoing as ever. The best time to mingle with them is during the wind-down *passeggiata* gap in the late afternoon, when people stroll around their neighborhoods, visiting each other on the streets and in cafés to shed the cares of the day and prepare for the evening of bliss ahead. This is when and where you'll feel what an Italian community is truly like.

So, please don't hold back when you fall in with a local crowd (because, let's face it, you will). Italians usually greet each other warmly and in a somewhat formal way. Such introductions will likely consist of a handshake with direct eye contact and maybe a smile. If a man and a woman are greeting each other, the woman often puts her hand out first.

Avoid any awkward entanglements by refraining from shaking hands over the top of other people's hands because theirs are either dirty or wet. Instead, nod and apologize.

Do not be frightened of il *bacetto.* Although bestowing this air kiss on both cheeks (starting with the left) may cause many Westerners to blush, it is pretty common in informal settings like reunions among family and friends.

The standard, more casual verbal greeting is *"Ciao"* (Hi), but instead, some people may say *"Buongiorno"* (Good day) or *"Buonasera"* (Good evening) if they want to be more formal. You must always address a stranger by their title and last name until invited to transition to a first-name basis. Older generations prefer to be addressed by the more respectful *"Signore"* (Mister) and *"Signora"* (Missus).

Dining Etiquette

It's over the dinner table where you'll want to know the script by heart. Before we dive into the specifics of what could be on the menu in each local region, the following tips apply to all restaurant outings and must be observed when appropriate.

Courses Are Served Individually

So much can change between courses: the subject of conversation, mood, appetite. This is why Italians order their courses one at a time rather than all at once, and they will expect you to do it this way as well. Why? You won't be tempted to devour your delicious dinner all at once. Instead, you'll have time to savor all the intricate combinations of flavors and personalities you'll encounter.

Napkins on the Lap

In Italy and many other countries, it is proper to place the napkin on your lap as soon as you sit down (and loosely on your chair if you must leave the table during your meal). After eating, fold your napkin to the left of your plate to signal to the server that you've finished your meal.

No Elbows on the Table

According to a Bible passage in the Book of Sirach (Ecclesiastes) (n.d.), "stretching your elbow at dinner" is disrespectful to the host. Whether or not this religious reference is the real reason behind Italians' distaste toward placing elbows on the table, try to rest only your wrists on it with your arms at your sides.

Water or Wine Over Soft Drinks

Drinking a glass of cola between forkfuls of delicately prepared fusilli will overpower the taste of the dish. Traditionally, water and wine are the preferred beverage choices since they are often more suitable complements to meals than sugary carbonated drinks–although sparkling soda water (*acqua frizzante*) is also popular. Your server may recommend different wines with specific dishes, as the various flavors will make for a fruitful pairing.

Wait Until Everyone's Food Arrives

Food is the nucleus around which social occasions in the Bel Paese revolve, so eating there is an experience meant to be shared. Therefore, it wouldn't be polite to take your first bite before all have been served. Once everyone's plate is in front of them, "*Buon appetito*" ("Enjoy your meal") will be your cue to begin.

Pass Food to Your Left

Sharing dishes is my favorite aspect of eating with others. This also forms the basis of a complete Italian meal. Shared plates like appetizers (*antipasti*) and bread with seasoned olive oil and vinegar are passed around the table to the left so everyone can enjoy them.

Don't Stack Your Plate

To finish off the perfect Italian meal, by the end, you should see your reflection glowing back at you from the sheen of your empty plate. Stacking your plate in a restaurant is rude since it may be interpreted as a sign that you did not enjoy your meal. Serve yourself only as much as you can eat, leave the rest for others, or if it truly is too much, ask for a box to go (*pacco da asporto*).

Cheese Etiquette

Contrary to popular belief, cheese does not suit all Italian dishes. Therefore, if the food is served without cheese, it's best not to ask for it.

Don't Switch Your Fork and Knife Around in Your Hands

Italians do not switch knives and forks. Instead, hold your fork in your left hand and your knife in your right. You may get a nasty shock when you find your plate no longer there if you place both utensils across it when you excuse yourself from the table (this is the signal to the waitstaff that you are finished). Putting your cutlery on either side of the plate lets them know you are still eating.

When you have finished your meal, place the knife and fork parallel to each other diagonally across the right side of your plate, with the tips pointing to ten o'clock and the handles resting at four o'clock. Your server will understand the sign and clear away your plate.

For Pasta

The way you eat pasta will depend on the type you order. For long pasta, like tagliatelle, use your fork and spoon to twirl the pasta around your fork. Once you get the hang of this rotation, you'll find it to be a more practical method of eating that also helps you prevent sauce stains on your shirts! With shell pasta like penne, you can still use a knife and fork.

Don't Bite Your Bread

Chomping your way into a loaf of crusty bread while dining is to be avoided. First, it makes a mess, and second, it's impolite. The best way to enjoy bread with your meal is by tearing off smaller, more manageable pieces.

Don't Rush Your Meal

If you're looking for an express dinner, reconsider going out to eat at a restaurant anywhere in Italy. The concept of "grab-and-go meals" is long gone; while you're in the Bel Paese, the art of doing nothing (*il dolce far niente*) is the only pitstop you'll have to make time for.

But make no mistake—eating in Italy is not viewed as "doing nothing"; it is recreational. Food is seen as so much more than mere sustenance, so it should be no surprise that most large meals can last several hours at a time!

Enjoy your dining experience by easing into the various courses of pasta, meats, and desserts. This is what your vacation should be about: taking your sweet time. They don't call it the sweet life (*la dolce vita*) for nothing!

No Smoking Allowed at the Table

Between 2002 and 2004, the European Commission unanimously enacted a ban on smoking in all public settings, including entertainment venues like restaurants and bars. Therefore, smokers are expected to excuse themselves to smoke outdoors.

Paying the Bill

A simple way to indicate readiness to pay is to casually wave your hand or gesture with your left palm flat while pretending to write on it with your right hand.

European Tipping Etiquette

Tipping is less common in Europe than in some other parts of the world. Nonetheless, it is customary to leave a small tip (typically 10–15%) for exceptional service.

Unwrapping the Joys of Giving

When you feel it is appropriate to bring along a small gift to show your appreciation, keep these tips in mind:

- If someone gives you a gift, open it in front of the person once you've received it.
- Deliver gifts in decorative wrapping paper. However, avoid black or purple paper; these colors symbolize mourning/grief for many Italians who are more traditional.
- Many locals believe it's bad luck to receive a knife or pair of scissors as a gift, so be sure not to give these to anyone. Perfume is also not a good idea since it sends a message to the recipient that they are emitting an unpleasant odor.
- Locals often appreciate receiving a gift of alcohol - but not specialty foods - from your home country.
- It is in poor taste to disclose the gift's price. Always remove or cover the sticker price.
- If you are giving flowers, remember that chrysanthemums symbolize death and are used at funerals, while red roses are meant as a romantic gesture.
- Gifts of homemade food are treasured as some of the best presents to bestow since they come across as a labor of love.
- New Year's, Epiphany, Valentine's Day, Mother's Day, Father's Day, Carnevale, Christmas, and Name Day (Onomastico) are all appropriate occasions to exchange gifts. More to come on festivities in the following sections!

CULINARY DELIGHTS FOR ALL TASTES

While pasta and risottos (*risotti*) are available throughout the country, the spice of life truly kicks in at the table of an authentic regional meal. True, no matter where you might find yourself seated, your host or server will attempt to convince you that gorging on plate after plate of pasta is, in fact, part of a well-balanced diet.

If you're dining at a *trattoria* (informal restaurant), be on the lookout for any long, glass-shielded counters displaying the antipasti that are available. This ingenious trick will make any traveler's eyes outgrow their stomachs!

The essence of a quality Italian meal boils down to its simplicity: local fish grilled with a few stalks and fronds of fennel, along with vegetables sautéed with little to no elaborate disguise. If Bella Italia truly does provide a sense of theatrics, then food may be the one thing with no glitz whatsoever; it's merely a labor of love. Allow me to transport you from one region's menu to the next as we make our way from top to toe of the country's uniquely shaped geography.

Food in the Northwest

Aosta Valley

Generous servings of melted Fontina cheese (not to be confused with the fondu just a stone's throw away across the Swiss border) top boiled cornmeal to form *polenta concia*, a Courmayeur favorite. Another tasty authentic regional dish to sample is *carbonada*, a stewed meat with wine, onion, and spices.

Piedmont

Turin cuisine is most famous for its aristocratic *bollita* dish of boiled beef with sausage, chicken, white beans, cabbage, potatoes, and a red *pomodoro* (tomato) sauce.

Liguria

A quintessentially Ligurian dish is *pesto Genovese*, made with basil, pine nuts, olive oil, garlic, and Parmesan cheese. Pair this with the region's native pasta, *trofie*, at Trattoria Rosmarino. For coffee and cake, try the reconverted palace (*palazzo*), Cambi Café, located in Genoa's Sacripantina.

Lombardy

The paddy fields hugging the Po River up north have long made rice a rival to its fellow carbohydrate staple—pasta. If you find yourself there, don't hesitate to order *Risotto alla Milanese*, featuring slow-cooked rice saturated in white wine, beef marrow, and butter (not oil). It should be dusted with a bit of saffron and Parmigiano Reggiano cheese as it is served.

Milan has another culinary claim to fame: *costoletta* (which puts a worthy spin on Austrian *schnitzel* and Polish *kotlet schabowy*, respectively). This pan-fried breaded cutlet can be prepared using chicken, veal, or beef.

Food in the Northeast

Veneto

When meandering along the canals of Venice, do not be alarmed if you see someone smacking cod flesh against a gondola's mooring post to tenderize the fish. For the real Veneto experience, follow this sighting up with a dinner of cream of salt cod (*baccalà mantecato*). Each bite will surely transport you back a few hours to that fateful moment!

Emilia-Romagna

The packaged *salami* (the plural of *salame*—sausage) you find in super-markets is most likely mass-produced in Milan. For the real deal, visit the city of Ferrara for a taste of its spicy sausage cooked in tomato sauce (*salame da sugo*).

With a name like Bologna, ignoring your suspicions about the link between Emilia-Romagna and the famous Bolognese red sauce may be difficult. Historians have since cleared up any confusion by confirming that the earliest ragù sauce was made in the 18th century in Imola (just west of Bologna).

This foodie city is where you'll find Eataly FICO, an entire theme park devoted to Italian food and agriculture! Plus, Emilia-Romagna is where Parmigiano Reggiano cheese, Parma ham (*prosciutto di Parma*), balsamic vinegar, and mortadella Bologna all originated. When talking to locals, be sure never to refer to slices of this delicious sausage - which dates back to ancient Roman times - as "baloney!"

For transcendent pasta, stop into Pasta Fresca Naldi for an authentically hand-made takeout—unless you manage to snag yourself a stool at the chronically busy restaurant.

Too often, the city of Parma is overshadowed by nearby Bologna unless someone brings up the subject of prosciutto di Parma. This heavenly ham reflects so much of Parma's identity that above the main cathedral's door, you can find a 15th-century engraving of a man killing a pig for its flesh. There is just no way you can escape this city's rich culinary heritage.

Parmigiano Reggiano is another spell-binding ingredient–a secret well kept by its "PDO" production, which protects Parma's right to produce this hard cheese. Be sure to sample *tortellini in brodo*, a local Emilia-Romagna favorite. The pasta is filled with prosciutto, Parmigiano Reggiano, and other ingredients and then served in a fragrant chicken broth.

Food in Central and Southern Italy

Lazio

Literally translating into "jump in the mouth," the originally Roman dish, *saltimbocca*, is just too tasty to resist. This veal escalope would not be complete without being wrapped in strips of prosciutto, sage, and a dash of lemon. When in Rome, don't wander too far from Navona Square (Piazza Navona) to taste-test this local favorite.

An authentic local spin on traditional spaghetti pasta is known as *pici*. This variation on the classic is much thicker and typically cooked with a wild boar meat bouillon (*pici al ragù di cinghiale*).

Umbria

Umbrian cuisine offers a culinary feast for all tastes. While visiting Castelluccio di Norcia, taste the local lentil soup and the region's Pecorino cheese. The area surrounding the national park is also known for its white truffles, which are almost always used as seasoning in the town's cheeses, pasta, and cold cuts like boar meat salami and Ciauscolo.

Tuscany

In Florence (Firenze), vegetarians will appreciate the local signature *ribollita* vegetable stew, *acquacotta* cabbage, bean soup, and the mouth-watering combination of baked beans with herbs known as *fagioli all'uccelletto*. Contemporary variations of this region's delicacies are served at Michelin-starred Gucci Osteria da Massimo Bottura in Florence's Gucci Museum (Michelin, 2024).

Campania

Since the 17th century, the king of Neapolitan ingredients, the tomato, has reigned in the Campania region. With their powerful kick, these juicy gems have dominated what is arguably the nation's greatest culinary invention: pizza. A stop at Pizzeria Brandi is required for pizza pilgrims; there, you will find a plaque commemorating this historic place where Pizza Margherita was first made. The classic version is topped with the colors of the Italian flag: red tomato sauce, white mozzarella, and fresh green basil leaves. Another popular, local variation of the classic pizza is the second greatest Italian culinary creation: a pocket-sized calzone folded over into a half-moon. Gino Sorbillo Pizzerie Napoletane has you covered.

In the south, you can get even the night owls out of bed at a reasonable time just by uttering the magic word: *sfogliatella*. Paired with a cup of strong coffee (brewed in Naples's distinctive pot, the *cucumela*), this classic croissant, filled with sweet ricotta cheese, will rouse even the most stubborn sleepers to breakfast.

A visit to nearby Sorrento will be your actual Italian "when life gives you lemons" moment. Groves of these oversized, tangy fruits are cultivated all along the town's cliffs overlooking the Bay of Naples. One grove worth visiting is near the Villa Massa Limoncello Distillery, where the Massa family has produced its version of the iconic lemon liqueur since 1890. In Sorrento, lemons are a part of daily life, from squeezing one over your catch of the day to being infused into a pastry or zested, aged, and chilled into a refreshing glass of limoncello. Taste Sorrento's golden secret for yourself with a reservation at "The Museum of Hospitality," Ristorante O'Parrucchiano La Favorita.

The Islands

Sardinia

Sardinian cuisine is a mix of several distinct Mediterranean flavors and ingredients. The region's traditional *semolina fregula* pasta contains accents of North African *Berkoukes* balls. Native Cagliaritans like to whip up their classic fish stew (*sa cassola*) and roasted eel (*anguidda arrustia*). Seafood lovers should book their reservations early at L'Imperfetto or Sa Piola, both found in the old quarter, Il

Castello. There's no better place to feast on marine delicacies than by the sea!

Sicily

In Sicily's capital of Palermo, Spanish, Arab, and Greek inflections are as fragrant as ever. Expect to see swordfish and sardines by the boatload, along with the city's devotion to its many ways of serving eggplant, from eggplant parmesan (*parmigiana di melanzane*) to *caponata* salad.

A dinner at Trattoria Ai Cascinari to taste all of this magic won't let you down, but if you're out and about exploring the Norman Palace or the Cathedral, take advantage of the souk-like markets on Carini Gate Street (Via Porta Carini) to get nibbling on a cone of fried rice balls (*arancini*).

Wine and Culinary Pairing

The stuffy "wine connoisseur" stereotype can sometimes scare off the less well-acquainted, whose taste buds might benefit from a good pairing of food with a fine Italian *vino*.

At their core, the best combinations match the richness and texture of the cuisine with the body of the vintage. It's all about the balancing of flavors. Like an artist mixing the different aromas on your palate, think about how they can bring out the best in each other.

As an example, savory cuisines bring the vino to a milder taste, while sweet foods often intensify it. Also, a light sparkling selection will cleanse the palate when paired with a saltier entree.

In this section, we'll go over how to eat and drink like a true Italian!

Red Wine and Italian Food Pairings:

- Cabernet Sauvignon

This bold, rich wine is made from the Cabernet grape. Shortened to "Cabs," the grape's flavors include bursts of black currant, some notes of blackberry, and even overtones of mint.

Cabernet Sauvignon's heartiness goes well with many tomato-based sauces in pasta and pizzas, as well as with fatty red meats like sirloin and ribeye steaks. This red also nicely complements the earthiness of mushrooms, lamb, and most cheeses.

- Chianti

It certainly wouldn't be a catastrophe if all Chianti wines were produced in the Bel Paese! The Chianti area itself is in the heart of Tuscany and enjoys a worldwide reputation for making the best vino to pair with Italian cuisine. Very dry (which means "not very sweet") but with a bold acidity, this red brings out the best in salads, dishes made with cheese, and red tomato sauces.

- Pinot Noir

Pinot Noir red wine is well known among foodies for its delicious pairing with oil-based dishes and red and white pasta sauces.

White Wine and Italian Food Pairings:

- Sauvignon Blanc

Sauvignon Blanc, which means "wild white" in French, is believed to have roots in France's Loire Valley and Bordeaux regions.

This white wine is known for delivering a clean, tart, refreshing flavor. Depending on its ripeness, this can veer toward overtones of green apple, lime, peach, and passionfruit. Sauvignon Blanc pairs well with parsley, basil, rosemary, mint, cilantro, and many other ingredients!

- Chardonnay

Chardonnay works well with creamy dishes like pasta Alfredo or lighter proteins like clams and chicken because it won't overwhelm their flavors. The grape can release tropical flavors like papaya and passionfruit if grown in warmer climates. You'll feel punches of apple, peach, and pear in Chardonnays from cooler regions.

- Pinot Grigio

Also labeled as Pinot Gris, Pinot Grigio was first produced in the Bel Paese. Its minerally, dry, and light-bodied flavor profile finishes with a crisp tang, making this refreshing selection an excellent accompaniment to light pasta sauces, risottos (*risotti*), and seafood.

FESTIVALS AND EVENTS: A TAPESTRY OF TRADITIONS

Although connections to traditional regional and religious festivities have dwindled throughout the 21st century, many of these celebrations are kept alive by and for the tourist trade. Across the four seasons (*quattro stagioni*) and 20 regions, Italians let off steam during public holidays–more often an excuse to have a party just for the sheer fun of it. And rightly so; there is so much to celebrate!

Here is my comprehensive (though not exhaustive) guide to the festivities in Italy year-round:

Winter

January 1: New Years Day (Capodanno)

After a night of ringing in the new year, taking the day off to rejuvenate and sleep in is only natural. While some places might still be open, it's best to double-check since most will be closed. Ice bath enthusiasts will be pleased to learn that there's something for them this time of year. Venice even holds an annual New Year's swim in its lagoon!

January 6: Epiphany (Epifania)

This Catholic tradition marks the 12th and final day of Christmas, commemorating the arrival of the three wise men at the birthplace of baby Jesus to bestow their gifts upon him. Any late hints of Santa Claus are forgotten the night before as children gleefully await the coming of La Befana, a witch on a broomstick who fills their shoes or stockings with candy or coal.

Though most stores and markets will be closed, the streets will be far from quiet as parades and street fairs swing into action. Sometimes, the boat races of Venice even feature racers dressed head to toe as the Leading Lady herself!

February: Carnival (Carnevale)

Italians take advantage of Carnevale's window of indulgence before abstaining from "the good life" during the 40 days of Lent. Sweets are served up while anthems blast out at parties. In Venice, lavish masks and costumes careen up and down the streets even weeks before the actual celebration, making the Floating City *the* place to be for Carnevale. The date varies each year depending on when Easter falls.

Spring

April 10: Sicily's Procession of the Mysteries

Sicily's Holy Week during Easter Time is perhaps its most famous of all, particularly for its Procession of the Mysteries, which symbolizes the passion and death of Christ. This line of 20 floats representing Jesus's suffering is paraded throughout the city from Holy Souls of Purgatory Church (Chiesa delle Anime Sante del Purgatorio) on Good Friday, followed by lights and emotional crowds to its return on Black Saturday. First held in 15th-century Trapani, this event is one of the world's oldest and longest, lasting a staggering 24 hours!

Easter Sunday: Florence Remembers Pazzino

The tradition of Scoppio del Carro ("explosion of the cart") celebrates the life and legacy of Pazzino, who came from Florence's esteemed Pazzi family.

Pazzino was the first knight to scale Jerusalem's walls during the initial Crusade, earning him three stone fragments from the Holy Sepulchre. Upon his return to Florence, the brave soldier used them to start a Sacred Fire before the people.

Nowadays, in a reenactment of this iconic scene, a large wagon filled with fireworks and drawn by oxen begins a circuit of the city in Porta al Prato. Locals also don 15th-century costumes for the occasion.

Sparks fly as the historic stones are used to light a string attached to the cart outside, all while Giotto's Bell Tower proudly sings. Get there early; this free event is very popular!

The Day After Easter: Pasquetta

On Easter Monday (Pasquetta), the music and wine keep flowing. Italians cheer up at the idea of a day off work during this public holiday when meet-ups with friends and family are happily required! While you'll see that most tourist attractions are open, why not do as the locals and go on a picnic instead?

The 2nd or 3rd Week of April: Verona's Vinitaly

The world's largest wine convention, Vinitaly, welcomes lovers of all things *vino* to Verona for four days of learning, sampling, purchasing, and networking.

April 21: Rome's Birthday Celebration

As classical legend has it, a gentle she-wolf once discovered two baby brothers. Little did the wolf know that these twins, Romulus and Remus, were the disfavored sons of the Gods. A disagreement broke out between the pair when they were old enough to debate how best to found a city. Romulus eventually slew Remus and went on to create Rome in 753 BCE.

When in Rome, do as the Romans do–and on the city's birthday, there can be no excuses! On April 21, you'll see everything from *tracciato del solco* (a trench-digging spectacle that honors the goddess Pales) to mock fights involving ancient Roman gladiators. The day concludes with a parade that begins and ends at the Circus Maximus.

April 25: Italian Liberation Day and St. Mark's Day in Venice

In a country with just 160 years of national unity as well as memories of the devastation of Mussolini's dictatorship, sharing the joys of public celebration inspires the locals to show their community spirit. April 25's Liberation Day (Festa della Liberazione) marks the end of the country's horrific experience during World War II under the Nazis.

Concerts, food offerings, political events, and other public activities commemorate this significant event. You'll see the date of this holiday marked on many street signs throughout the country, and businesses also close early.

The patron saint of Venice, St. Mark, also happens to host his feast day on April 25. There's no better way to commemorate the eternal spirit of Liberation Day's hope and St. Mark's teachings of unity than with a Venetian gondola boat race (*regatta*) and a massive party in St. Mark's Square (Piazza San Marco).

May 1: Labor Day (Festa del Lavoro)

May 1 marks Labor Day, which was first observed in the late 1800s during the labor movement of that time. Festa del Lavoro reminds everyone of the sacrifices made by generations of workers to improve working conditions, establish fair wages, and ensure social justice in the workplace. It still acts as a wake-up call to thousands of union activists dealing with present-day struggles for equality.

In Rome, the day ends on a high note with a large concert organized by the nation's leading trade unions. Expect the closure of major museums and limited public transportation.

Second to Last Sunday of May: La Cavalcata Sarda in Sardinia

Birds are chirping, and bees are buzzing next to newly bloomed daffodils. Meanwhile, the Sardinians are swooning over the freshness of spring and, without fail, hold one of their most memorable events in Sassari: The annual Sardinian Horse Race (La Cavalcata Sarda). Falling on the second to last Sunday of May, racers wear traditional clothing and ride their horses to the track for the main event.

This two-day extravaganza marks the moment in 1899 when King Umberto I visited Sassari to unveil the Square of Italy (Piazza d'Italia) and shows Sardinians' deep pride in their culture.

May-November: Venice Biennale (La Biennale di Venezia)

This international exhibition, held in several places around the city in even-numbered years, features the visual and performing arts in multiple forms. It also offers visitors the perfect opportunity to see the magnificent private apartments and villas where the expos are held. Check out La Biennale di Venezia's official website to learn all the details of their massive program.

May 15: Festa dei Ceri in Gubbio

The folkloric Festa dei Ceri in Gubbio is an annual tribute to the city's patron saint, Ubaldo, as well as two others. Every year on May 15, people lug three gigantic wooden candles (*ceri*) as part of a procession from the center of town all the way up Mount Ingino to the Basilica of St. Ubaldo. Together, all three candles weigh one metric ton (2,204 pounds)!

May: Venice's Vogalonga Regatta

By now, you've probably guessed the importance of regatta boat races down the Floating City's waterways!

Venice's Vogalonga Regatta is a non-competitive race for rowers of all abilities. What began in 1974 as a peaceful protest against lagoon degeneration and wave damage caused by motor boats has evolved into an annual celebration of the city's environment through some of its most scenic parts.

Today, more than 5,800 boating enthusiasts row over 1,500 boats along the 18.6-mile (30-kilometer) route.

June 2: Anniversary of the Republic (Festa della Repubblica)

June 2, 1946, saw the nation's democratic decision to do away with the then unfavorable monarchy and replace it with the current republic. Although the grandest celebration of Festa della Repubblica is in Rome, you are more than likely to stumble across some version of this festivity wherever you are in the country. Fortunately, the majority of tourist attractions stay open on this day.

Mid–June: Festival of St. Ranieri in Pisa

When the remains of St. Ranieri were placed in an urn at the Chapel of the Coronation (Cappella dell'Incoronata) in Pisa's Cathedral in 1688, a feast was organized while the river Arno and city streets awakened to candlelight by twilight, in an event known as Luminara.

In the annual commemoration on June 16, the buildings along the Arno are illuminated by thousands of lights and candles. Fireworks accompany this magnificent spectacle, which comes to a close on the river with a boat race the following day.

Summer

Ravello Festival

This celebration of the arts brings even more culture to the Amalfi Coast each summer. While throngs of tourists sweat under the burning sun, music lovers take refuge under the shaded gardens and banquet halls of the historic Villa Rufolo, where artists from a variety of disciplines showcase their talents. Also featuring art, dance, and other events, Ravello has it all!

June–August: Sicily's International Festival of Arts in Taormina

Like Cannes, Taormina Arte brings the best of cinema with a week of premieres and photo shoots. Beyond the silver screen, this art festival showcases plays, music, and dance performances throughout the summer.

June–December: Taormina Opera Festival

Taormina's annual opera extravaganza continues from the art festival. World-class singers perform in the Ancient Theatre (Teatro Antico) surrounded by a stunning backdrop featuring the rocky coast and dramatic Mount Etna. Tickets to see classics like *Carmen* and *Don Giovanni* can be purchased (at reasonable prices) either online or at the box office at Congress Palace (Palazzo dei Congressi).

June–September: Summer Opera at the Arena di Verona

That balmy breeze blows as the distant sounds of opera waft down the lanes in Verona, and that can only mean one thing. Each summer, Verona's incredible (and affordable) summer opera comes home to its equally jaw-dropping Arena, which is simply spectacular.

Early July and Mid-August: Siena's Palio dell'Assunta

The Palio horse races (Palio dell'Assunta) are held twice yearly in an ancient pageant whose history stretches back to the 15th century and before. The August contest tends to be the most famous, as this date is just before the national Ferragosto holiday.

Vibrant Renaissance-costumed knights and pages proudly display the flags of Siena's 17 parishes (*contrade*). This culminates in a bareback horse race around the Square of the Field (Piazza del Campo).

9–10 Days in July: Jazz in Perugia

Each July, Perugia's cobblestoned streets become home to the world's best-known jazz players. Get into the swing and blues of this fantastic Umbrian event!

Middle of August: Feast of the Assumption (Ferragosto)

From this date, restaurant and shop owners proudly twist their signs to "closed for vacation" (*"chiuso per ferie"*) in preparation for the three(ish) weeks of "doing nothing." The Feast of the Assumption commemorates Mother Mary's rise into heaven, thus marking the start of the country's annual rest period. To avoid getting caught in traffic or the swarms of buzzing vacationers (both local and foreign), it's helpful to avoid popular destinations during these few weeks.

Fall/Winter

First Sunday of September: Regatta Storica in Venice

For centuries, the legendary city on water has preserved one of its oldest traditions: the Historic Regatta (Regatta Storica). These boat races pay homage to Venice's unique watery environment; there's even an under-10s category! The most popular one is the Champions on Gondolas (Campioni su Gondolini), in which smaller, more agile gondolas zip down the Grand Canal to claim victory. Be sure to snag a canalside spot if you happen to be in Venice on this day!

First and Second Week of September: Venice International Film Festival

While its counterparts in Cannes and Berlin reel in thousands of movie buffs each summer, Venice's version completes the "Big Three" international film festivals with a bang!

This extravaganza began in 1932 and was originally part of the Biennale. Its activities and screenings are hosted in none other than the Cinema Palace (Palazzo del Cinema) on the island of Lido. If you're the type of movie fan who wants to see the best movies before the masses ever hear of them, then this festival is for you.

October–November: Harvest Festivals (*Sagre*)

October and November offer the abundance of the harvest season, and with that comes Bella Italia's delicious food festivals (*sagre*).

Typically organized around a single seasonal ingredient, sagre give thanks for the pleasures of the earth and prepare attendees for the changing of the seasons. The most famous ones are in Piedmont and Umbria for truffles, in Tuscany for chestnuts, and in Puglia for olives.

October (10 days, dates vary): Eurochocolate in Perugia

All things chocolate are sure to rivet the senses during a visit to Perugia's Eurochocolate, one of the largest such festivals in Europe. Since 1993, this annual sugar rush of tastings, cooking classes, performances, chocolate-sculpting displays, and chocolate markets always leaves candy addicts craving more!

November 1: All Saints' Day

This Catholic holiday celebrates saints known and less well known to spread blessings and good luck throughout the coming year.

According to pagans, this day marked almost a unity between the living and the dead since it was when the veil separating each was at its thinnest. Churches hold prayers to draw attention to the beings trapped in purgatory, followed by charity work and informal services in homes.

Since the dead are believed to return, houses are left vacant so loved ones can join the festivities during meal times. Contrary to common belief, this is not a time of doom and gloom; instead, it's filled with the sensational aromas of homemade specialties like beans of the dead (*fave dei morti*) and a quince gelatin dessert (*cotognata*). On All Saints' Day, death is celebrated, not mourned.

December 8: Immaculate Conception

For Italians, this Catholic holiday commemorating the Virgin Mary's conception of Jesus also marks the official start of the winter vacation season.

Feel free to be extra jolly this weekend as Italians decorate their trees and put up their lights all around the Bel Paese while holiday markets start cropping up everywhere. Restaurants and bars also tend to fill up fast, so make your reservations early!

December 24–26: Christmas Eve, Christmas Day, and Santo Stefano

If you're in Bella Italia on Christmas Eve, feel free to attend a holiday Mass. You can also pause for a moment of quiet reflection in almost any town. In many of them, the locals take great pride in crafting intricate nativity scenes, particularly in Assisi, where decorations are lavished everywhere. Some scenes may even feature live people and animals!

Keep in mind that most businesses and tourist attractions are closed on Christmas Day and the day after on St. Stephen's Day (Santo Stefano), so if you want to eat out, choose and reserve a spot well in advance–or be sure you're prepared to eat in.

EXPLORING ITALY'S ARTISTIC HERITAGE

Museums and Galleries

Little needs to be said about the ongoing pressure "not to miss" or to "be sure to visit" the country's many centers of cultural art. Sometimes, simply being among Italians can be as enchanting as spending an afternoon in the company of Bellini or Caravaggio's tableaus, for example. But, to the eager eye, these masterpieces are captivating nonetheless!

Uffizi Gallery (Galleria degli Uffizi), Florence

Paintings from the Bel Paese and throughout Europe are on display in the U-shaped Uffizi Gallery, where you can admire works by Giotto, Botticelli, da Vinci, Michelangelo, Raffaello, and other greats.

Located in Uffizi Square (Piazzale degli Uffizi), the gallery is just one of many other free or discounted (10% off) attractions included with the Florence (Firenze) Card.

Now, onto some of the showstoppers! The constant reshuffling of room numbers will make it impossible to pinpoint the exact locations of these two standouts. However, the gallery still arranges the pieces chronologically from the 13th to 18th centuries.

In his *Madonna Enthroned* (1300), Giotto breathes new life into a common subject in Renaissance art: the Madonna and Child. The artist's experimentation with perspective through contrasting light and dark (*chiaroscuro*) creates visual depth that stays true to the bond between the divine figures illustrated.

The sharp details in Titian's *Flora* (1515) make us probe into the many connotations shown on the canvas. The intricacies are undoubtedly Titian, from the sumptuous mantle draped over Flora's left arm to her pensive expression. I encourage you to ponder this singular portrait as long as time allows.

Accademia Gallery (Galleria dell'Accademia), Florence

An essential adjunct to Uffizi is the Accademia Gallery (Galleria dell'Accademia) in the City of Lilies. This museum first served

Florentine fine art students in 1784, and today, the education continues for visitors from all walks of life.

Michelangelo's seven statues draw hundreds of curious minds each day. It's a testament to the high Renaissance pioneer himself that his marble sculptures still hold such power despite six left unfinished (four *Prisoners*, a *St. Matthew*, and a *Pièta*).

Those with a penchant for antique musical instruments can also immerse themselves in the more modern section of the exhibition, which features fascinating pieces created by some of the greats, including Antonio Stradivari himself.

Vatican Museums (Musei Vaticani), Vatican City

At their best, the popes and cardinals at the Vatican's helm historically followed hot-headed military conquests with moral leadership; at their worst, they could show the same passion for political status as any Roman emperor. A visit to the Vatican's museums has much to teach the devoted and skeptics alike.

No matter how often you've heard the name "Sistine Chapel" tossed around during conversations with art history enthusiasts, for once, their embellishments are justified. Nothing will ever prepare you for the utter brilliance of Cappella Sistina, created in the 15th century. Keeping watch over its hundreds of daily visitors is the incredible *Last Judgment* (1536-1541), completed by Michelangelo over four grueling years. Before his work on this masterpiece, the artist had mainly been a sculptor and had completed only a few oil paintings. When Pope Julius II, who was then overseeing the works, laid eyes on the magnificent fresco, it's no wonder that he chose not to follow through with his threat to throw Michelangelo off the 46-foot (14-meter) scaffold!

Although often overlooked in the face of Michelangelo's masterpiece, the 15 rooms in the Picture Gallery are well worth an extra hour of contemplation. Among the most important are works by Giotto, Fra Angelico, and Raffaello's last great work, *Transfiguration* (1516–1520).

Capitoline Museums (Musei Capitolini), Rome

Rome's history is on full display in the Capitoline Museums (Musei Capitolini)! Be sure to catch the fascinating multimedia installations included in the many exhibitions.

Moving past the Garden of Villa Caffarelli (Giardino di Villa Caffarelli), you'll be greeted by a life-size reconstruction of the Colossus of Constantine (Colosso di Costantino). This 42-foot (12.8-meter) high statue, built in painstaking detail based on ten known fragments of the original from the 4th century, was unveiled in 2024 and is perhaps one of the most memorable in the Capitoline collection.

By the way, the café and restaurant on the top floor of the Musei Capitolini boast a fantastic 360° panoramic view of the city.

National Roman Museum (Museo Nazionale Romano), Rome

The National Roman Museum, established in 1889, safeguards one of the world's most significant archaeological collections, which is spread across four locations: Massimo Palace by the Baths (Palazzo Massimo alle Terme), Altemps Palace (Palazzo Altemps), Balbus's Crypt (Crypta Balbi), and the Diocletian Baths. Constructed around the year 300, the Diocletian Baths accommodated up to 3,000 visitors simultaneously. Picture bathers moving from the hot room (caldarium) to the warm room (tepidarium) and cold room (frigidarium) surrounded by magnificent stone walls adorned with colored marble.

Borghese Gallery (Galleria Borghese), Rome

Once home to the noble Borghese family that first moved to Rome in the 16th century and included a Pope, a Cardinal, and generations of patrons of the arts, Galleria Borghese reigns over 80 hectares of artfully manicured gardens and parkland. This mansion-museum contains paintings and sculptures crafted by Canova, Titian, and Bernini.

Egyptian Museum (Museo Egizio), Turin

Turin's Museo Egizio is second in importance only to the Egyptian Museum of Cairo. Near the Palace of the Academy of Sciences (Palazzo dell'Accademia delle Scienza), the Museo Egizio is the world's oldest museum of Egyptian art, history, and culture. It features Pharaohs of 1500 BCE along with mummified combs, crocodiles, and even foods!

Royal Museum (Musei Reali), Turin

Turin's hold over the peninsula boomed in the 17th and 18th centuries. This era also saw a radical transformation in the city from practical designs to the building of majestic Baroque structures. It's easy to see these historic changes and the age's panache as you move among the Royal Museum's large complex of buildings and exhibitions.

Echoes of a certain French palace may reverberate in the back of your mind as you tour the gardens of the Royal Palace here. That may be because the architect, Jules Hardouin-Mansart, was employed by King Louis XIV to design similar grounds around Versailles in Paris.

End your time in Turin with a visit to the Armory, where you can inspect lethal weapons dating back to the Etruscans.

Brera Art Gallery (Pinacoteca di Brera), Milan

This famous Milanese art museum contains the original of iconic Romantic painter Francesco Hayez's *The Kiss* (1859). Beyond its portrayal of young love, the artist created an allegory of the Italian unification movement, Risorgimento, through his intentional color choices. The gentleman's red stockings, the green lapel on his cloak, and the blues and whites of the lady's gown all allude to the link between Italy and France that helped to create the Bel Paese of today. Although Hayez painted other versions of Risorgimento housed in various European collections, the original retains its timelessness. As part of an initiative of the Ministry of Culture, the museum offers free admission on the first Sunday of each month and select holidays with a reservation.

Peggy Guggenheim Collection (Collezione Peggy Guggenheim), Venice

The unfinished 18th-century palace of Venier dei Leoni is home to the Peggy Guggenheim Collection. It was named after the American heiress whose admiration for Picasso, Jackson Pollock, Mark Rothko, Henry Moore, and even her husband, Max Ernst, can now be fully appreciated by the public. Ms. Guggenheim is even buried there, so her connection to the Collection will live on into eternity.

MUSE Science Museum (Museo delle Scienze), Trento

MUSE is a top choice for both adults and children. All six floors cover a single theme, ranging from prehistory and dinosaurs, sea and marine creatures to mountains, glaciers, and Alpine biodiversity. There's even a tropical greenhouse! MUSE's multisensory activities will enlighten and entertain just about any visitor.

South Tyrol Archaeological Museum (Museo Archeologico dell'Alto Adige), Bolzano

Ötzi the Iceman takes center stage at Bolzano's South Tyrol Archaeological Museum. By chance, a pair of tourists mountaineering in the Senales Valley found this Copper-age mummy in 1991.

The exhibition does a superb job of reimagining what must have been an incredible life from more than 5,000 years ago. Let your curiosity run wild as you explore Ötzi's activities, health conditions, diet, clothes, and hunting tools.

National Archaeological Museum (Museo Archaelogico), Naples

Thanks to the Museo Archeologico, the Campania region's treasures have miraculously been safeguarded from the ravages of the area's violent earthquakes. This collection is not merely a heap of dry bones and stones; its fascinating presentation should be where all visits to

Pompeii or Herculaneum begin and end. Pompeii's vibrant mosaics and Herculaneum's bronzes from nearly 2,000 years ago are displayed on the mezzanine floor. The ground floor is dedicated to sculptures, the most famous of which is *Doryphorus*, the Spear-Carrier of acclaimed classical artist Polycletus. The paintings housed here, with their astounding concentration of color, are undoubtedly some of the best preserved of any from ancient Rome, considering their rich history. The frescos of Terentius Neo and his wife almost emerge from their vertical plasters to come to life in vivid blues, greens, and those inimitable Pompeii reds.

Architectural Wonders

Nowhere is it easier to get your fill of museums, monuments, and places of worship than in Italy. It would, however, be a shame not to bask in the splendor of at least one iconic landmark–if only to say I came (*veni*), I saw (*vidi*), and I didn't-like-it-but-still-conquered (*vici*ed) it.

As Victor Hugo notes in his novel *Notre Dame de Paris*, "Architecture was the great book of humanity, the chief expression of man in his various stages of development, whether as force or as intellect" (1831). I would argue that architecture *is still* the crowning achievement of humankind, documenting the evolution of our cultural history. So, go forth, fearless adventurer, and read the paths of Bella Italia as if they were lines and its buildings as if they were words of printed text. The history engraved in these famous structures will keep you wondering about the nation's many cultural phases for a lifetime.

Rome's Colosseum

Here, you will see and feel the eternity of Rome. Aristocrats, merchants, artisans, and plebeians all passed through the 76 arched passageways (*vomitoria*) to see starved lions and tigers pitted against mighty gladiators and criminals in fights to the death on the dirty stage of the Colosseum below. Moss now grows in the crevices of the underground maze where men and beasts alike were once funneled to their graves.

Venice's St. Mark's Basilica (Basilica San Marco)

The familiar silhouette of Basilica San Marco, the city's patron saint, lies on the eastern side of St. Mark's Square. The building's exquisite design–so different from all the other churches of Venice, and indeed, Italy in general–harkens back to the city's historic role as a unique crossroads between cultures of the East and West. Once a chapel for the Doges–the highest officials in Venice–where the remains of Mark the Evangelist (St. Mark) are said to have been buried in 830, the basilica was reconstructed during the 11th century as a symbol of the age's blending of cultures. Mosaics from Byzantium encrusted the basilica's bold Islamic-style domes that continue to loom high over the church's Greek cross floor plan today.

The history behind each of the church's five portals deserves its own chapter—there is so much to be said. Before reading up on it, though, I encourage you to make your first visit with fresh eyes. Only then will you begin to build your own unique connection to this grand place of worship.

Monreale Cathedral (Duomo di Monreale) in Palermo

The 12th-century cathedral of Monreale is perched on a hilltop south-west of Palermo in Sicily. The building's influences were from entirely different cultures, so its interior matches its exterior only in grandeur. The outside boasts an interlacing of Gothic rose-colored windows, while the classical figures portrayed through the Byzantine mosaic depictions allow you to experience two worlds at once.

Old Bridge (Ponte Vecchio) in Florence

The little houses that cling to the rear of the arcade of boutiques in Florence's Old Bridge (Ponte Vecchio) have good reason to do so. Intact since 1354, this was Florence's first and, for centuries, its only bridge. In an attempt to slow any advances during the Allies' invasion of 1944, the Nazis chose to spare Ponte Vecchio and destroy several other bridges instead.

In 1966, the temperamental Arno River decided to change course. On November 4, the river broke free from its banks to flood the city, taking with it 1,000 paintings, 500 sculptures, and numerous precious books and manuscripts. If it had not been for the public rescue operation, even more treasures would have been lost.

All the more reason for Ponte Vecchio's inhabitants to hold on for dear life!

Milan's Cathedral (Duomo)

The pinkish-white marble hues of the Duomo of Milan dominate the robust façade (finished in 1813) of this magnificent achievement. Nowhere does a cathedral have such a hold over a city as this one does in Milan. The magical moments you share during your evening stroll (*passeggiata*) through Piazza del Duomo (the square at the cathedral's footsteps) will pull you deeper into the lovely spell it's cast for centuries.

Like most colossal structures, this building boasts a mix of cultural influences. Beginning in 1386, teams of Italian, French, Flemish, and German architects and sculptors collaborated to create this one-of-a-kind marvel. For an unbeatable view of the city, wander high above the hustle and bustle by ascending all the way to the roof!

The Leaning Tower of Pisa

With only 300 years to stay (somewhat) erect, the Leaning Tower (*campanile*) is one of the nation's busiest tourist spots. Everyone wants to see it before the structure's unstable subsoil gives way. I recommend scaling the 294-step spiral staircase to gaze out over the city from 183 feet (55.8 meters) above.

Rome's Pantheon

This "Temple of All Gods" is so reminiscent of ancient Rome that it rivals the Colosseum in its prominence. Its builder, Emperor Hadrian, broke through countless barriers to achieve this triumph of design and engineering in 120 CE, giving its coffered dome an overall interior diameter of 141 feet (43 meters), which is even larger than St. Peter's Basilica.

National Museum of 21st Century Arts (MAXXI)

MAXXI, the National Museum of 21st Century Arts in Rome, stands out as a beacon of modern Italian architecture. Designed by Zaha Hadid, an Iraqi-born architect, this remarkable structure was unveiled in 2010, showcasing a bold and innovative design. Through iconic achievements like MAXXI, the country's architectural narrative evolves beyond its historical roots. According to its website, "MAXXI represents an awareness of the importance of promoting the current creative expressions of a nation such as Italy" (MAXXI, 2024).

STEPPING STONES...

Experience Italy like a local at the table, during social occasions, at festivities, and feeling awestruck while visiting its many landmarks. As you wander the streets, pondering the various influences every corner seems to display, remember to keep your eyes open, and you'll be reading Bella Italia and its culture in no time. It's funny how our experiences of certain places will shift depending on who we're traveling with–or perhaps with no one at all! Wherever and whatever context you're traveling in, remember to ground yourself in the present moment. Connect with all the life that's around you.

In the next chapter, we'll address some specific needs of solo travelers, women and female-presenting individuals, members of the LBGTQIA+ community, and families in the Bel Paese.

CHAPTER 6
NAVIGATING SOLO, LGBTQIA+, AND FAMILY ADVENTURES

> *Veni, vidi, vici* – I came, I saw, I conquered.
>
> JULIUS CAESAR

SOLO TRAVELERS' HANDBOOK

"But don't you get bored?" an acquaintance leaned over to whisper to me as our small talk broached the subject of solo travel–namely, my recent experiences on the road that month. The crumpled napkin on the table between us seemed to open into full bloom; I couldn't stop staring at it while deciding what to say.

I had to think about it. At the time, I was still learning the ropes of traveling alone because, let me tell you, there are plenty to wrestle with. Still, the love I have for solo travel is unparalleled. Some of my warmest memories were created during nights out by myself in new environments. The satisfaction might not fill you up the first time or even the second, third, fourth, fifth, or sixth time you spend long periods with only yourself for company. But if you're really into it, I urge you not to give up. Trust me, the journey is what counts (sometimes even more than the destination itself), and it's one filled with wonderful people. Ironically, if you're lucky, you may find yourself becoming more attuned to others than if you were exploring as part of an already established group. Being alone reveals the value of being with others and sharing experiences, and it'll push you to make more and deeper connections.

Beyond the safety tips covered in Chapter 2, this section will walk you through the more personal aspects of traveling solo. I hope to debunk any unreasonable perceptions we may have learned from the dreaded "social norms," if only to empower any adamant soloists out there who may be reading this and thinking, "I've felt that way, too!" The road is long and stretches far and wide; remember that it's yours and yours alone. Walk it with ease!

Anxiety

So, you've decided to go it alone. The anxiety you're feeling almost makes you want to pull a 180, run out of the airport, and catch the next ride home. Not so fast! Remember to breathe. Let's take a moment (if we have time before check-in closes, that is) to sit down and run through a couple of facts. Remember how confident you were in booking those flights, organizing your accommodation, and even getting your visa in time? Try to think back to updating your friends and family on your travel plans. Is the anxiety you're feeling right now connected to reality, or is it a by-product of the story you're telling yourself?

For reasons I am still grappling with, society at large is not always as understanding of those traveling solo as it is of couples who go off together on vacation. Socially speaking, most people are a little intimidated by those who can hold their own, although they'd never admit it. Why? I suspect that they're just insecure. Feeling confident in one's own skin—confident enough to cross the globe alone—may trigger those who perceive themselves to be stuck in body, mind, or circumstance. Although we crave it, freedom is more readily accepted as a concept than a practice. My belief (and lived experience) is that solo traveling can single-handedly break through these barriers. As soloists, nothing and no one is tying us down, and we are completely removed from the limits placed on us in our daily lives.

So, feel free to take a few moments to recalibrate and come back to center. This will bring the intensity down for you during those moments of panic as you explore the world on your own.

Questions You May Like to Consider:

- How do I view solo travel?
- What do I see as my ideal trip?
- What can I do to make myself feel better now?

Loneliness

After emerging victorious from the first mental battle while checking in, you have successfully boarded your flight, and suddenly, the turquoise Mediterranean waters sparkle at you as you glance outside the plane's window. Before long, it's sundown as you stroll through the quaint cobblestone streets of your new favorite city. Lovers pass, hand in hand, quickly followed by groups of friends laughing their heads off at some inside joke. You check your phone screen, meaning to call a friend or family member, but your trip has placed you in a different time zone. They're probably busy.

And then the loneliness kicks in. Feeling isolated while you're abroad can sometimes be the most challenging part of solo travel–even more than flight delays, indecisiveness, and getting lost. Like the ecstasy you might feel as you fall in love with a city, this lonely feeling is only one other part of the same journey. Don't be afraid to embrace it, no matter how self-contradictory that feels. Travel, in general, has gained such a glamorous reputation; social media shows post after post of smiling faces against lush backgrounds. And while some of those images might be real, they don't paint the *full* picture. So, try to avoid scrolling on social media if you're feeling alone while traveling; it won't give you the perspective you need to overcome these hurdles. Instead, stay active. Plan itineraries, get in touch with any local connections you may have (close or distant to you personally), and talk to people if you feel that will help. Journaling may also work to give you some much-needed clarity.

One final tip: If this will be your first time traveling solo (or even traveling in general), consider booking a shorter trip of two to four days to test the waters. While some might like to dive right into the deep end, others prefer not to get in over their heads just yet. Solo travel is an exercise in independence that many (myself included) are still learning, even after years of globetrotting.

Questions You May Like to Consider:

- Is there something I am lacking at this moment? If so, how can I satisfy this need in the here and now?
- Am I truly missing them, or am I just bored? This one might sound a bit brutal, but hey, you're on vacation, so give it a chance anyway.
- What can I learn about myself from this experience?

Eating

The magical fairy lights wrapped around the branches shading the restaurant's patio are too surreal to resist. Before the waiter even asks, you politely gesture and say *"per uno"* ("for one") in that perfect Italian trill you've been practicing, and suddenly, those solo blues are cast off. You sit outside among the locals, whose chitchat melds into the background noise accompanying your first glance at the menu. Just then, the pang returns, but this time, it hits you hard between the ribs. Why does the idea of eating a perfectly decent meal alone feel this way sometimes?

True, it might not be for everyone, but eating at a table "for one" is becoming increasingly popular, especially among women and female-presenting individuals. I say "increasingly popular" because, again, like the stereotype of solo traveling, the perception of women "doing things alone" has long been criticized and even feared–but more on that in the Empowering Solo Women and Female-Presenting Travelers section later in this chapter.

Personally, I find eating out alone very enjoyable. My life is quite hectic, so I savor these me-time moments, particularly over a hot dish of pappardelle and a glass of red. If you're curious and have never done it, the only way to find out if it is for you is to try it. It's not the end of the world if you don't enjoy it; there's always a Plan B takeout option that you can ask of your server, along with an early payment and quick exit.

If eating in a restaurant or café seems too much, consider a public spot with a good view, like a park bench, beach, or harbor. One night in Salerno, I must have spent around three hours straight boat-watching, my legs dangling on the dock. I still remember the peace I felt in those moments.

Dinner clubs are popping up in many European cities. If eating out alone is getting a bit boring during your trip, scan the Web for a group meal near you. These events can be fantastic ways to buddy up with like-minded travelers while sharing a culinary adventure!

Budgeting

A solo meal on the first night of your trip may not be what you need right now. That's fine, you tell yourself, making a mental note to return to this same restaurant on a different night. You can even get it to go! You signal for the bill, which arrives in Italian time: no rush at all. No matter—you're on vacation; you're supposed to be relaxed. So, why, then, is your heart racing as you do a double-take at the total? It can't be that much, can it?

Well, it can. The picturesque string lights dazzled you, dispersing all thoughts of coperto, the usual ten percent cover charge. The place was excellent, and you were prepared to pay for a modest appetizer and entreé, but not coperto, and not that bottle of water.

Every single one of these scenarios has happened to me at some point while traveling. Each situation is challenging in its own way, but when it comes to money, those feelings that follow can seem even more troubling. Just know that everyone, experienced or not, will run into at least one money-related problem abroad, so you are not alone in your worry. The bright side is that you'll live to see another day, and when that day comes, you'll be more prepared. Then, the day will come when you'll give budgeting advice to friends embarking on their own solo travel adventures.

Since you know yourself best, budget according to your needs and tastes–and don't forget to ask about coperto and request a jug of tap water (*acqua dal rubinetto*). Some might say it's a travel faux pas, but there's nothing wrong with drinking perfectly potable water from Italy's refreshing aqueducts. Try to maintain a reasonable balance. Don't be afraid to treat yourself on occasion, but make those moments count!

Connecting With Other Solo Travelers

There's nothing like sharing experiences with fellow travelers and, in some cases, even the locals themselves. These moments often feel like they've been pulled right out of a Greta Gerwig movie, and you may just have to pinch yourself. Random connections formed abroad can be one of the best parts of traveling solo, yet it's often far easier said than done. Let's face it: you've already come this far, both physically and emotionally (because, yes, it does take courage to fly solo), so why not take that extra step and even be willing to make the first move? Stay open to learning more through new experiences, and I promise that your glowing energy will bring good vibes back to you!

Here are some ideas for how to spice up your social life in Bella Italia:

Stay in a Hostel

Most likely, if you're staying in a hostel, you'll meet like-minded globetrotters traveling on a budget, too. Stay open and start chatting if you feel like there may be a good vibe going. Being friendly to fellow visitors is generally a good idea no matter where you're staying. But, if you're the type of person who likes your own space, your needs might not be so easily met here. The bottom line is to choose places to stay that support your goals for the trip and are within your budget.

Share Your Food

If you're in a shared accommodation, everyone's plans for the day can be a fun topic of conversation at breakfast. Maybe you'll find out that the person sitting across from you at your hostel in Rome is just as excited about seeing the Colosseum and the Vatican Museum as you are!

Try on a New Persona

You're going to new places and trying new foods, so why not try a new persona, too? Put yourself out there and say yes! You can dress differently, use Italian words you've just learned, order something for dinner that catches your eye on the menu, or go out to that club you've heard others rave about. This is the time to be your best self– the Italian vacation version, that is!

Take a Class or Workshop

The Bel Paese is packed with creativity, and there are plenty of ways to find out if any classes or fun workshops are happening while you're in town. Chances are, if you attend something you're really into, you'll have no problem finding at least one solid person who shares your tastes. Try asking your host for advice, searching for your interests in your favorite search engine, following accounts on social media, or keeping an eye out for flyers in shop windows as you roam the city streets.

Use Meet-Up Apps

Likewise, it's possible to use meet-up apps to stay in the loop. Often exclusively considered "dating" apps, some have not yet come into the mainstream. In reality, many people using these apps are "open to making friends" as long as they list this on their profiles. Don't rule out the potential for apps to help you do this, too, or if you're looking for it, maybe something a little more romantic!

Join a Live Event or Bar Crawl

If you're a night owl and want to socialize after dark, why not look for a bar hosting live music performances or even search for larger concerts nearby? You can also always bond over a beer or two (or three!) on a late-night bar crawl.

Join a Group and/or Walking Tour

Head over to the tourist office and book a tour in your language. It might sound a bit cliché, but these types of events will draw you closer to like-minded people—and if not, at least you'll be learning more about this fascinating country!

Learn The Language

A little can go a long way, especially when it comes to language. If you're open to striking up a conversation with locals, most of the time, communication in Italian (even if it's a little broken) will immediately break the ice. This is because it shows people that you're interested in them and their country and don't mind going out of your way to engage. Not only does it speak volumes about your character, but it can flatter the person, and there's no harm in that! (*Flip back to Chapter 4 if you need a refresher on essential Italian words and phrases*).

Remember, these experiences can only take shape with a kind, calm, and confident demeanor. You want the people around you to feel like you're open to getting to know them.

Here are some tips on how to be (safely) approachable:

- Try minimizing your use of electronics. This will ground you in the present moment, making it easier for you to meet new people.
- Plus, the less you're on your screen, the more your open body language will attract others to you. So, remember to keep your head high and smile if that feels right for you.
- Try to let things unfold spontaneously. You never know who you might be sitting next to on the train. Perhaps they're reading that book you just finished and have been dying to share your thoughts on.
- Don't slouch. Actions speak louder than words, as the saying goes. The same can be said for body language. Sitting up

straight shows that you're open to meeting and getting to know others.

Perfect Solo Spots

Any city will look and feel different depending on who you're experiencing it with. This is why I've compiled a list of destinations that can be thoroughly enjoyed solo–all well-connected, compact, and utterly beautiful. (*For more in-depth info on some of these destinations, see Chapter 5*).

Anghiari

Not as popular as many other Italian locales, the village of Anghiari in Tuscany is a safe bet for peace and quiet. Da Vinci based his famous work *Battle of Anghiari* on the real one fought in 1440 between the Florentines and Milanese, only for the painting to be lost and then brought back to life by copies, which are now on display at the Uffizi Gallery in Florence. Revel in the spirit of Anghiari at the Museum of the Battle (Museo della Battaglia di Anghiari), Galbino Castle (Castello di Galbino), and Sarci Castle (Castello di Sarci).

Bologna

Apart from being one of the world's most titillating food destinations, Bologna is a perfect place for solo wandering. Many of its basilicas and squares are within walking distance of the historic center.

Courmayeur

You can't go wrong with time spent in Courmayeur, located in the Aosta Valley. Ski on its Alpine slopes, indulge in a relaxing visit to the spa, and warm up with a hot drink at one of its classic cafés. Then, take a ride on the Skyway cable car to see Mont Blanc up close.

Cinque Terre

The diversity of Cinque Terre also makes it an accessible solo travel spot. When you get bored with sunning yourself, the most popular way to get around is by hiking on the 7.5-mile (12.1-km) Blue Path (Sentiero Azzurro) connecting all five villages. Wind your way through vineyards and past ancient fortresses as you gaze out onto the coast of the Ligurian Sea.

The Etruscan Coast

These 54 miles (87 km) from Piombino to Livorno are perfect for you if you like nature and are looking for some R&R on your solo adventure. The beaches on the Cecina coastline are simply gorgeous. If you're interested in learning more about local marine life, the Livorno Aquarium (Acquario di Livorno) is a must-see. Or, for an unforgettable experience of Etruscan history, look no further than the Archaeological Park of Baratti and Populonia (Parco Archaelogico di Baratti e Populonia).

Florence

Florence is so packed that if you think you might be prone to spouts of loneliness, it will chase those blues away!

There, you'll find a classical yet modern ambiance teeming with social activities, from cooking classes to walking tours and wine tastings. And if you'd like to whisk yourself away on a day trip, Pisa, Bologna, or rural Tuscany are all accessible by train.

Milan

Milan offers an unbeatable experience for soloists who are especially interested in retail therapy. Dive right in by visiting the oldest Italian shopping mall, Galleria Vittorio Emanuele II. The huge cross-shaped arcade harkens back to the region's 19th-century commercial prowess.

Once the sun goes down, if it feels right, then take a tour with like-minded souls to see an entirely different side of this fabulous city.

Naples

Are you worried about eating at a restaurant alone? Then Naples is the place for you. Eating out somewhere a little more relaxed is part of the city's culture. You'll see people munching on a slice of pizza by the harbor or maybe snacking on a sweet treat on the steps of the cathedral (Duomo).

Orvieto

This pit stop between Florence and Rome has a small-town feel. It offers affordable accommodations, along with excellent food and wine options. Its friendly vibe creates the perfect atmosphere for solo travelers to chill for a few days.

Ostuni

In the region of Puglia lies the "White City" of Ostuni. The effect of this sea of white buildings next to a sky of blue is nothing less than magical. You will love this city on a hill, which offers spectacular views of the Adriatic Sea nearby, delectable delights like local cheeses and wines, and a central location close to many other popular places.

Padua

Padua combines Orvieto's relaxed vibe with its own rich arts and cultural scene. Once you've explored what Padua has to offer, its convenient location will make for easy connections to Venice, Verona, and Vicenza.

Recco

Recco, on the Ligurian coast, is the perfect place for surfing. Beginners from all over the world will love this place for its beauty and patient instructors. Contact Blackwave Surf School for more details.

Rome

Stay in Rome's historic downtown area for the best opportunity to visit some of the world's most famous landmarks on foot. This area is very safe, so you can take your daily morning cappuccinos on the Spanish Steps or Navona Square (Piazza Navona) in total peace.

Craving company? Join one of Rome's many food tours and taste your way through the city with other foodies.

Sappada

Would you enjoy an Alpine village where it feels like time stands still? An ideal destination year-round, Sappada is just that place. Its 1,300 residents, who still speak a local Germanic dialect, will welcome you as you enjoy summer hikes, winter snowshoeing, festivals, and a visit to their Ethnographic Museum.

Trieste

Where the Adriatic Sea meets Northern Italy, you will find the city of Trieste. Known by coffee lovers for its vibrant café culture, it's easy to get around here on foot. Don't miss the historic Borgo Teresiano district, Miramare Castle, or a visit to the statue of famous Irish writer James Joyce.

Tropea

This seaside town–the pearl of the Tyrrhenian–is perfectly situated in Calabria in the south. Here on the Coast of the Gods (Costa Degli Dei), the snorkeling, especially at the beaches of 'a Linguata, Cannone, and Rotonda, is breathtaking. In town, you'll find locally made handcrafts (including coral jewelry) to take home as souvenirs or gifts.

Valbruna

In the northeast, also near the Alps, lies the town of Malborghetto-Valbruna. Perfect for hiking and biking, Valbruna is a nature lover's paradise. Pay a visit to nearby Lake Bled, just over the border into Slovenia, for a view of historic Bled Castle or a boat ride to see the Church of the Assumption (Chiesa dell'Assunzione di Maria). If you're there in October, check out Valbruna's annual Ein Prosit food and wine festival.

Venice

Wear your most comfortable walking shoes and prepare to lose all sense of space and time as you wander around the 150 canals that flow through the Floating City.

Verona

Travel to Verona solo for an unforgettable getaway. This city is ideally located for independent travelers, with only an hour-long train ride to neighboring Bologna (or less).

Vicenza

Vicenza's breathtaking natural beauty will be all the company you need on your solo trip to Bella Italia. Recharge your social battery at the Oasis of the Valley of Silence (Oasi della Valletta del Silenzio) parkland, just a seven-minute walk from the city center.

EMPOWERING SOLO WOMEN AND FEMALE-PRESENTING TRAVELERS

It's strange to think that in this modern era, the idea of women traveling alone can still come as a surprise more often than I would like. For centuries, women's movements have been closely monitored by the state, society, and family, which was seen as being for good reason. Over history, women, especially when unmarried, were generally seen as second-class citizens who lacked the means to defend themselves against the sordid realities of life. Only through marriage (or a connection to some serious wealth) could women be safe from discrimination, and even then, life was still dire.

Today, things have changed; women have the right to vote, and most also have equal access to property, divorce, abortion services, etc. Sadly, this is not the reality for all women, and we, as a species, will never reach true freedom until we are all considered equal.

However, the stigma of traveling solo as a woman still remains. Much of this concern stems not only from a fear of staying safe amid the unpredictability of certain social situations while abroad but also from women's lack of self-confidence.

Go to Chapter 2 for tips on how to stay as safe as possible while you're in Italy. There, you can read up on how to plan ahead, especially when going out at night.

A Well-Deserved Confidence Boost

It's a topic that often comes up at the table with my girlfriends whenever we get together: solo travel as a woman. "Why should it be any different?" asked Maya, a friend of mine. I remember her look of complete nonchalance as she shrugged off all the imagined complications concerning the idea of women traveling alone. She was correct; why should it be any different, at least when it comes to the things we can control? Instead of constantly second-guessing if we look weird or seem out of place doing something, shouldn't we try to make life easier for ourselves and do it regardless of other people's opinions, which are totally out of our control?

Having time totally for yourself is something to be grateful for. Think of your relationship with yourself as being just like a relationship you might have with a friend. You make so much time for them, so why wouldn't you like to make that time for your own peace of mind?

Traveling abroad often involves extensive research. The more you learn about the best places to visit, the more prepared you'll feel. When planning your itinerary, I recommend organizing your day around a main activity like a tour or a museum. That way, you'll be able to strike a pleasant balance between being spontaneous and having direction. Maya puts it best: "If you can survive at home, why should it be different elsewhere?"

Take that risk, and I doubt you'll be disappointed. Before I started traveling, I was so skeptical of even the most minor interactions with others. For the most part, the people I've interacted with have often shown themselves at their best. I couldn't say how often I've had to rely on the goodness of strangers to get out of sticky situations, sometimes even for money to buy a last-minute bus ticket back to my hotel!

LGBTQIA+ Adventures

The first time I went solo traveling in Italy was in Rome. I was presenting and still present as an openly Queer woman, though at the time, I felt most comfortable in a buzzcut, flannels, and piercings–the whole shebang. Growing up, it was common to face homophobia on a daily basis. So, when I took off to Rome on my own, first as a tourist, one of the first questions I asked was, "Will I be safe?"

The answer depends on where you go. Milan, Rome, Venice, Florence, and other cities of similar size will feel like most popular ones do (with their own unique charms, of course), while smaller, more rural areas may feel a little harder to navigate. That's not to say, however, that you should totally avoid all the lush greenery Italy has to offer. It's just something to anticipate so that you can prepare for the worst while always expecting the best!

In the Bel Paese, you'll find many places where the Queer community is brimming with life. Here are the places I've been where I felt most at home:

Rome Conquers

Over thousands of years, the Eternal City has undergone countless life cycles, with empires falling only to regenerate and grow anew. Today's Rome isn't much different. Its vibrant, inclusive energy makes it a perfect travel destination for Queer folks and Allies alike!

One particularly welcoming place you won't want to miss is Trattoria da Cesare al Casale. Nestled in the heart of Rome, this family-run business is a well-known gem, loved for its warm hospitality and authentic cuisine.

Countless books on Renaissance art history have shamelessly declared that Michelangelo was "married to his art," conveniently skidding around the subject of his romantic attractions. Wrong. Michelangelo was gay, and the Vatican, which owes so much to his incredible work, should be proud of it. Since 2015, anyone interested in the Vatican's heritage has been able to enjoy an art tour with Quiiky to gain fresh insights into the real identities so closely associated with the Church, with one of the most important being Michelangelo himself.

One of the highlights of Pride Month is the acclaimed Roma Pride parade. If you're in town, join the festivities and connect with the local LGBTQIA+ community for the best experience. There's also Gay Village–an annual summer festival that turns Nymphaeum Park (Parco del Ninfeo) into a vibrant LGBTQIA+ hub. With live performances, DJ sets, food stalls, and art installations, GV radiates good vibes. If you don't get a chance to visit in the summer, don't worry–some alternatives are open year-round. Some showstoppers are My

Bar, Coming Out, and Company Roma, all located within walking distance of the city's center, and the Alibi Club for drag shows.

Catania Calls

Sicily is buzzing with a dynamic LGBTQIA+ community. Glam up (in whatever style you like!) when taking Catania's Gay Street by storm near the Alessi steps or dining at restaurants like Via Alessi or Nievski.

This city also has a strong association with LGBTQIA+ movements. Founded in 1980, Arcigay Catania is Italy's first and largest gay activist community. They often run events and workshops at their headquarters on Verona Street (Via Verona). Follow them on social media for the latest.

June brings the legendary Gay Pride parade to the city, along with its classic wash of rainbow colors.

On the corner of the road that curves southeast of Catania's Cathedral Basilica of Saint Agatha (Basilica Cattedrale di Sant'Agata) stands an old Red Tree (Arvulu Russu in Sicilian dialect). Since the 1930s, this has been the most popular meeting spot for Bella Italia's gay community. Some experiences are chronicled in the book *La Città e L'Isola* (The City and the Island) by Tommaso Giartosi and Gianfranco, Goretti, which explores the Queer culture and hopeless romances during the era of Mussolini's fascist regime and the wartime tragedies (2006). The iconic tree continues to attract thousands of intrigued visitors each year.

Bologna's Rainbow

As one of the first Italian cities to open a center protecting gay rights, dubbed the Cassero LGBTQIA+ Center, Bologna has long been active in putting measures in place for the Queer community. Since 1982, there have been many local events, including Gay Pride, workshops, conventions, and drag nights.

The city is filled with places that have contributed significantly to its Queer identity. Here are some highlights for anyone fascinated by this city's rich cultural heritage:

First, this Italian city bore two noteworthy LGBTQIA+ figures: Pier Paolo Pasolini, a renowned poet and filmmaker, and Lucio Dalla, a singer-songwriter whose ties to the community surfaced posthumously. Explore Cavour Square (Piazza Cavour), featured in Dalla's hit song *Piazza Grande* (1972). Pasolini's birthplace at Borgonuovo Street (Via Borgonuovo) is also worth a visit! At the Renzi Library of the Film Library Foundation of Bologna (Biblioteca Renzi Della Fondazione Cineteca di Bologna), you can indulge in the Pier Paolo Pasolini Research Center and Archive, housing most of his works. Or, stop by Villa Aldini, the backdrop for his controversial film *Salò*, or *The 120 Days of Sodom*, which challenged societal norms with its homoerotic undertones (1975).

Bologna also houses the arched Municipal Palace (Palazzo D'Accursio). This seat of the Municipality of Bologna and its institutional bodies was taken in 1990 by Marcella di Folco, the first openly trans person to hold public office as the Councillor for the Saragozza district. Pay this town hall-turned-art-museum a visit!

Continue into the Stefano Casagrande Gardens, which have been open within the medieval walls since 2012. This spot owes its name to one of the most ardent campaigners of the Bolognese gay movement. This artist-activist also contributed to founding Il Cassero, the Italian national organization for gay rights.

The year 2012 marked another notable Queer milestone: Saragozza Gate (Porta Saragozza) was chosen as the starting point of the National Pride Parade.

Florence: Historically Gay-Friendly

Florence holds the distinction of being the first Italian city to abolish the death penalty in 1786 and eliminate punishment for homosexuality in 1853. The Medici family, known for patronizing the arts, ruled the city from the 15th to the 18th century. Among them, Gian Gastone de' Medici, the final Medici Grand Duke of Tuscany, was openly attracted to the same sex.

Explore Florence's underground nightlife by descending into the medieval catacombs to find Tabasco, Italy's first gay bar, located near the Signoria Square (Piazza della Signoria). LGBTQIA+ travelers in Florence can seek assistance from AITGL (Italian Association of Gay & Lesbian Tourism), a non-profit organization established in 2009 to ensure the country is welcoming to everyone. This excellent resource offers tourist information and legal support.

Caravaggio, a prominent figure in LGBTQIA+ history, is known not only for his use of chiaroscuro at the Uffizi Gallery but also for his revolutionary artistic techniques. His mastery of contrasting light and dark elements solidified his reputation as one of the most sought-after artists of the Renaissance. There are speculations that Caravaggio, who was gay, engaged in a love affair with Mario Minniti, the painter believed to have modeled for *Bacchus*, one of Caravaggio's famous works on display at the Uffizi.

Milan Serves Up

With legendary soirées hosted by the Glitter Club, where nonconforming artists like Glitz Girls and the miraculous Myss Keta refuse to back down, Milan gives as good as it gets when it comes to strong LGBTQIA+ counterculture. Of course, this entails music, creativity, and all-around good vibes. How could you expect any less in the home of the Bel Paese's largest LGBTQIA+ community?

Venice Gate (Porta Venezia) has assumed status as Milan's "gay neighborhood" par excellence. As fate would have it, after Porta Venezia's subway stop was showered with rainbow murals during the parades of Pride Week in 2019, Milan's mayor decided to leave them there permanently as a tribute to the neighborhood's identity. Porta Venezia has several gay bars, including Mono, Pop, and Leccomilano. The intersection of Lecco Street (Via Lecco) and Panfilo Castaldi Street

(Via Panfilo Castaldi) is a celebrated meeting point for all LGBTQIA+ people where you will also find swanky bars and restaurants that are Queer-friendly. Be sure to check out an area known as NoLo, located in northeastern Zone 2. Diverse, welcoming, and edgy, it's no wonder this area is quickly becoming the city's next LGBTQIA+-affirming neighborhood. Give the Navigli District a visit for even more trendy bars and restaurants.

Opera fans will love La Scala (Teatro alla Scala), where the magic of this classic Italian art form will leave you with memories for years to come!

Beyond the glittering nightlife, you may want to continue exploring Milan's Queer culture by day. Read up on intersectional movements stretching from feminist discourse to Queer studies in Libreria Antigone (they also have a bookstore in Rome) and immerse yourself in MIX–Milan's celebrated Queer film festival. Sforza Castle (Castello Sforzesco) is a perfect place to tap into impressive art collections, some of which include pieces crafted by none other than the Renaissance Queer icon Michelangelo.

The Pull of Puglia

This region in Southeastern Italy borders the Adriatic Sea and has a very open, inclusive feel. I recommend renting a car so you can easily reach all the best spots. Starting in the south on the Salento peninsula, you'll find some of the best Queer hangouts and LGBTQIA+ community in Gallipoli ("beautiful city") and Taranto. The food here is spectacular, and the vibe is laid-back. While most beaches cater to everyone, head one hour north of Gallipoli to the country's best gay (and clothing-optional) beach, D'Ayala. Some other hidden gems are small towns like Alberobello, Lecce, Ostuni, Otranto, and Polignano a Mare.

Taormina Delivers

This eastern Sicilian town in the shadow of Mount Etna nevertheless casts a bright light of acceptance over the region. Warm people and comfortable weather abound here. Relax while shopping along Umberto Street (Corso Umberto), enjoying authentic cuisine at one of many restaurants, sunbathing at beaches like Giardini Naxos and Mazzarò, or swimming at Isola Bella. At night, sit down for a drink with people from all over the world at the popular gay bar, Shatulle. Looking for a place to stay the night? Try Isoco Guest House.

Tuscany's Finest in Torre del Lago

Waiting for your discovery in this famous region is a hidden gem of gay Italy–the town of Torre del Lago. Situated on the coast between the Tyrrhenian Sea and Massaciuccoli Lake, it is filled with well-cared-for gardens and even a museum devoted to iconic opera composer Giacomo Puccini, who called Torre home for much of his life. On the town's main walkway, you'll find gay bars like Mamamia (stay for its late-night parties and drag shows!), Baddy, and Piccolo Café. Check out the annual Mardi Gras celebration if you're here just before Lent. In the warmer months, you'll love beaches like La Lecciona (halfway to the nearby town of Viareggio and marked with a rainbow flag) and Le Dune.

The Amalfi Coast Amazes

With a length of 30 miles (48 km) and protected as an official UNESCO World Heritage site, the Amalfi Coast is picturesque, easy-going, and gay-friendly. Visit the romantic seaside towns of Positano and Amalfi for unforgettable cuisine and spectacular views. I recommend renting a car to easily travel between locations on the winding roads near the Coast or taking a boat to reach its secluded beaches and see its towering cliffs up close.

FAMILY-FRIENDLY ITALIAN ADVENTURES

The time has come for you to plan your family's getaway to Italy. Perhaps you've been worried about how you'll please everyone, so much so that the bliss of sitting in the Italian sunshine has slipped your mind. Not to worry! This section of the chapter will relieve the stress of catering to everyone's age, taste, and personality so that you can get back to feeling excited about the quality time you'll have together. *(Go back to Chapter 3 for a refresher on all the best Italian beaches, must-see towns, and other hidden gems)*.

Allowing time for more peaceful moments and reflection (even writing things down!) can be a great way to make the most of your family vacation. Remember, everyone in your family wants to have a good time and create lasting memories together. This isn't always easy, and challenges may come up. However, even those moments can solidify relationships and bring you all closer. So, just roll with it and make the best of your family's Italian adventure!

Traveling With Teens

If you're feeling slightly nervous about traveling with your teenager, you're not alone. The influences of social media and instant communication can sometimes make us feel like we're speaking different languages, which can be challenging to navigate. Plus, they continue developing into their own selves, which can sometimes cause conflict. Still, they'll be open to discussing the trip with you, no matter their personality or interests. After all, they'll want to have a great time in Italy just like everyone else in your family! Here are some tips to help things go as smoothly as possible.

Include your teen in preparing for your vacation by asking them what they want to do. Then, give them a sense of ownership by allowing them to plan some aspects. Why? This will remind them that it's their adventure as much as yours.

Setting healthy boundaries can also help keep things balanced. Don't be afraid to set some ground rules, particularly regarding screen time. If social media is a problem with your teen, clearly state your expectations for your time abroad and reach an agreement before the journey begins. Plus, since you've involved your teen in the planning process, you'll already have some leverage to negotiate.

Consider building in an amount of family hang-out time that you and your child are comfortable with. Then, schedule some alone time for them, too. I recommend not overwhelming them with travel education at every corner. A focus on learning is best kept for school field trips rather than a relaxing family vacation.

If your budget allows and your teen insists on it, consider letting them bring a friend. This added company may encourage greater independence and collaboration. It's also a great way of getting to know more about your teen as a person.

They're likely growing more independent, but that doesn't mean they no longer need your support for basic needs like having shoes and clothes that fit. Ensuring they're in the right gear will help them stay comfortable and make for a more pleasant vacation for everyone.

They'll be with you but will still want to keep in touch with others back home. Make sure their phone plan allows them to keep their friends up to date on all the fun they're having!

No matter where you're from, you and your family will represent that place to all the Italian locals you'll interact with. Help your teens to do their best to fit in through what they wear and how they behave.

Do they want to sleep in? Let them! Mornings can be the perfect time to enjoy something you've wanted to experience alone or with your partner. After all, this is your time to explore, too!

Yes, they're teens, but setting limits can still help them avoid packing too much and overspending. It's helpful to give them a budget for souvenirs and encourage them to leave some space in their luggage so all their favorite finds will make it home, too.

Postcards with stamps from the cities your family visits won't take your teen much time to write and will give friends and loved ones back home their own souvenirs from your family's trip!

Finally, I recommend encouraging them to keep a travel journal. This will help them reflect on events during their time in Italy that are important to them, and later, they'll look back fondly on their thoughts, feelings, and descriptions of new experiences they captured in those moments.

The Best Places to Go

Here are some of the best places in Italy to take your toddlers, tweens, and teens. To keep it simple and practical, I'll split the highlights of each region into two parts. The first will be for parents of younger children to tweens, and the second will be geared toward families in general but include activities for teens. Don't worry - no matter their ages, your children will love the vast array of natural wonders, arts, foods, and local cultures they'll experience in the Bel Paese!

Tuscany

Florence's Republic Square (Piazza Repubblica) boasts lively playgrounds that captivate toddlers, while older children revel in museum outings and exploring quaint, secure villages in Tuscany—a haven for children of all ages.

Still, you should avoid Tuscan cities if you're visiting in the hot months of July and August without a car–this would force you and your family to spend lots of time in sweaty crowds. It's best to visit cities like Florence and Pisa in the spring, fall, or even for the end-of-year holidays. Summertime is best for farm stays (*agriturismi*) or beach rentals. Italian heat means spending your days by the pool or beach before exploring villages and cities in the evening.

The ideal way to see the rolling hills of the Tuscan countryside is to rent a car (*visit Chapter 2 for an average price*) so you can drive out to the smaller villages and landmarks like the Abbey of San Galgano (home to the sword in the stone!) or Tuscany's hot springs. You might also want to stay in a city and take a bus to visit other nearby destinations. One of my favorites is a day trip from Florence to San Gimignano.

Where to stay? Agriturismi in the countryside are a fantastic option (*see Chapter 2*). Besides that, your standard hotel or beach rental on the coast or hotel/apartment in Florence or Lucca will do just fine!

Kid-Friendly Things to Do:

- Period costumes at Palazzo Vecchio: Book a kids' dress-up tour at Old Palace (Palazzo Vecchio), where children and adults alike can learn exciting facts about the royal history of Florence. (From around 23€ per adult).
- Scavenger hunt at the Uffizi Gallery: Introduce your children to the Bel Paese's rich artistic heritage with a fun and educational private tour of one of Europe's most important museums. A tour guide will accompany you and your kids on a treasure hunt while they search for hidden details in the masterpieces on display, like flying machines in some renowned da Vincis! (From around 63€ per person).

Activities for Any Age:

- Cooking Class: Immerse yourself in a pasta-making extravaganza during an afternoon cooking session at Diacceroni Experiences in rural Tuscany. With a wonderful 4.9-star rating, they offer a three-hour culinary experience led by skilled chefs. The cost is 75€ per adult, 30€ for ages 10-17, and 25€ for ages 6-9.
- Artisan Craft Tour in Oltrarno: Unveil the heritage of craftsmanship in Oltrarno, Florence, where generations have honed their skills. Witness master artisans at work and gain insight into their time-honored techniques. Prices start at approximately 373€ per adult.
- Bike Rentals: Explore Lucca on two wheels with bike rentals starting from 5€ per hour or 20€ for a full day. Cycle along the historic city walls for a fresh perspective on Tuscany's charm. This is a family adventure your teens will surely cherish!
- Soak Up the Hot Springs: Treat yourself and your teen to a spa day in the wild at one of Tuscany's most beloved natural springs at the Baths of St. Phillip (Bagni San Filippo).

Sicily

The beauty of Sicily is sure to enchant any visitor. However, I would avoid traveling with small babies, as the bumpy roads aren't particularly stroller-friendly. Also, think twice about traveling in the hot summer months because, trust me, even the most beautiful beach spots (*see Chapter 3 for some inspiration*) will start to feel overwhelming when you're among huge crowds.

To avoid being elbowed while sunbathing on the Ionian seashore, I recommend visiting in the spring, fall, or winter. Winter is one of the best times because it's quieter and less expensive, and the weather is usually still warm enough to take a dip, even in December and

January. Archaeological sites are also less crowded and not as sweltering.

Although Sicily has public transportation, it isn't always so reliable. My advice: rent a car in Palermo or Catania and explore on your own four wheels!

As with Tuscany, the Sicilian countryside is too charming to overlook, so I suggest booking a farm (agriturismo) accommodation. Hotels or apartments in Palermo, Taormina, or a town in Val di Noto are also available.

Siracusa boasts an enduring charm. Ruins dating back as far as the 8th century BCE lie beneath flourishing lemon and orange groves while café tables grace the vibrant Baroque squares (*piazze*). The city's historic structures seamlessly intertwine with medieval alleyways that unveil breathtaking vistas of the sea. Siracusa is smooth, even, and easily traversable, complete with traditional stores and tantalizing scents of gelato and Sicily's own sweet treat, granita.

The traditional puppet theater of Teatro dei Pupi brings stories of epic sword fights and dramatic beasts to life. You can stroll through history at the Neapolis Archeological Park to find one of the world's largest Greek theaters or enjoy the panoramic view of the city from the water on an exciting boat ride.

Kid-Friendly Things to Do:

- Palermo's Puppet Show: Mimmo Cuticchio's Puppet Theater (Teatro dei Pupi di Mimmo Cuticchio) will string you and your kids along into the colorful world of Sicilian folklore (*folklore Siciliano*). This unique traditional puppet theater is a must for those seeking light entertainment (email Figli d'Arte Cuticchio directly for prices).

Activities for Any Age:

- Visit Mount Etna: The easiest way to climb up the legendary Mount Etna with your kids is to get a professional to lead. Interactive tours come equipped with helmets and torches to help you explore Etna's lava flow cave, an utterly magnificent geological formation (*see Chapter 3 for more information*). (Average prices are around 71€ per person. Group rates may also be available).
- Food Tour: With flour up to your elbows, on a food tour, you and your family will make your own pizzas (*pizze*) and pasta and taste these delicious creations. When you're done, just be sure to loosen your belts a notch or two! (Inquire directly at Sicilian Food Tours for current prices).
- Visit the Papyrus Museum (Museo del Papiro): Introduce your kids to the fascinating history of papyrus. This tool once dominated Sicily when it was a crossroads between ancient Egypt and the Byzantine Empire. The biggest colony of papyrus plants in Europe once grew at the heart of the island of Ortigia in Siracusa along the banks of the Ciane River. This living museum is in constant evolution, and your kids can see how papyrus is produced and even take part in lab work! (Inquire for current rates by messaging the museum directly).
- Go For a Hike: Starting from the coast, venture further into the vast natural delights this island has to offer. Your teens will especially love the array of landscapes.

Dolomites

Travelers of all ages will love the fresh mountain air in the Dolomites. Share Northern Italy's incredible kid-friendly/stroller-friendly trails with your children in child carrier backpacks or even on foot. Exploring the Dolomite valleys on two wheels is also possible. Affordable road bikes, e-bikes, and baby bike trailers can all be rented by the day or longer (starting at around 59€ for a 2-day rental)

If dressing up and nightlife are your things, I would pass on this region since it's very low-key. You'll mostly find only mountain gear while shopping in the smaller villages!

I love to visit in the summer or winter. Spring and fall are "iffy" weather-wise, and while there may be snow on some trails in June, October can be sunny and bursting with the vibrant colors of the changing leaves. All my parent friends who've been here agree that winter is their favorite, not only for the kid-friendly snow sports but also for the country's best Christmas markets!

Local buses will get you to where you'll begin your hiking trip, but I recommend covering longer distances by car.

Adventure lovers in your family will thank you for staying in a mountain hut (rifugio), which can be reached by car or chairlift!

Activities for Any Age:

- Family Rock Climbing: Open to all levels, guided rock-climbing tours/lessons can be booked through Explore-Share for a full day of vertical scaling and stunning mountain views (starting from 93€ per person).
- Visit the Open-Air Museum: The Austrians built the Three Stones (Tre Sassi) fort between 1897 and 1901 in an attempt to block the Italian army from accessing Badia Valley (Val Badia). Guided family tours can be organized for as little as 9.30€ per person if you reserve in advance.
- Hike: Hikes through the Meadow of the Village of Siusi allo Sciliar (Alpe di Siusi) are packed with beautiful landscapes. There are trails for all levels. The freedom of being out in the open air is especially popular with teens.
- Go Horseback Riding: Explore the lush scenery of the Dolomites on horseback with your teens, who will definitely remember this unique adventure. Organize a tour with expert leaders for the best experience. (Prices will vary from agent to

agent, so get in touch with your selected operator directly for more information.)

Puglia

The south has some fantastic white sand beaches and quaint villages that are sure to keep everyone's attention.

For the best beach experience, visit in May, June, or September, and avoid July and August, when the seaside can fill up with crowds very quickly.

Unless you're staying at a beach resort and planning to stay there for your entire trip, I recommend renting a car so you can easily visit small villages and other beaches nearby.

If you've never slept in one of Alberobello's cone-shaped *trulli,* you need to get to Puglia quickly (*velocemente*)! Countryside fortified farmhouses (*masserie*) are also well-liked as an accommodation option.

Activities for Any Age:

- Caves of Castellana (Grotte di Castellana): Discover a network of white caves on a 1.8-mile (2.9-km) tour loop of underground caves. Guided tours can be arranged for around 151€ per person.
- Visit the filming location of James Bond's No Time to Die: Are your teens huge James Bond fans? Prepare to be shaken and not stirred as you visit Gattini Palace (Palazzo Gattini) in Matera, where the 25th film of the classic action series was filmed in 2020.

Rome

Rome is primarily a walking city, so if you're comfortable going a long way on foot with your family, it is definitely worth visiting. Of course, bringing kids aged five and up is possible, but the excursion may not be easy for them amid the sea of people, distances between monuments, and cobblestone streets (not always stroller-friendly). Tweens and teens will love exploring the city they've been learning all about in class. Likewise, vibrant areas like Trastevere and Monti won't fail to charm.

Rome is at its best when the weather is warm enough to eat outdoors without sweating through your outfit. You'll find the best times to travel there are in the spring (just not during Easter week) and autumn.

One essential thing to know about Rome: *Never* attempt to drive there. The Romans have their own ways of driving, which can take months or even years to get your head around. Moving around on foot is encouraged and very easy to do in this city, but if you need to give your legs a rest, those hop-on, hop-off buses work just fine, too!

Apartments or hotels in Trastevere or Monti near the Forum and Colosseum are well-situated to give you and your family a balance of downtime and staying active.

Kid-Friendly Things to Do:

- Scavenger Hunt in the Vatican Museums: This private tour is the perfect way to keep your kids engaged while uncovering the Vatican's hidden secrets through a treasure hunt. Booking through Secrets Italy will let you skip the line to get the adventure going faster! (Kids under four go free, 5–15-year-olds are 50€, and over 16s are at 60€).
- Attend Gladiator School: Train to be a gladiator at Rome's finest gladiator boot camps. This exhilarating two-hour crash course will teach you how to fight like a warrior of Ancient Rome as you learn what life was like in the imperial city. Gruppo Storico Romano's Gladiator School has even been graced by Shakira and actor Owen Wilson. (Starts at around 121€ per person).

Activities for Any Age:

- Bike the Borghese Gardens: In Chapter 5, we explored the fascinating history of this imposing mansion and its gardens. For an unbeatable experience, take your family on a bike ride around the 80 hectares of grounds. The bike rental stand is called Bici Pinico, and they charge 12€ per hour for a standard two-person ride or 20€ per hour for the four-seater Riscio Max.
- Become Amateur Archeologist-Historians: There is just so much to see in Rome that it can easily leave your head spinning. Why not cut out the stress and book a private tour around the city, giving you and your family a good foundation for understanding it? Many tours will cover classic Roman landmarks like the Colosseum, Palatine Hill, the Roman

Forum, and the Vatican (all with varying prices). You and your teens can share in this learning experience together!

- Go on a Vespa Tour: The sweet life (*la dolce vita*) doesn't get much sweeter than when you're zipping around one of Europe's most magical capitals. Depending on your teens' ages and experience, you and your family may opt for a self-driving tour or one with a driver. (Prices start from 144€ per person for a tour.)

- See a Football (Soccer) Stadium: Shoot a shot you're sure not to miss by planning a visit to Rome's legendary Olympic Stadium (Stadio Olimpico) on either a tour or (depending on availability) for an actual match. (Prices will vary for match tickets, so it's best to check the venue's official website for more information).

Venice

Venice is deceptively tricky if you have a child who's just learned to walk. Why? There's a lot of open water, large crowds, and no railings between the streets and canals. Although it can be done, it's exhausting for the adult in charge. I would recommend putting off a family trip to the Floating City if you'll be the only adult and you need to bring a stroller. It's tough carrying a stroller over all of the bridges.

I can't recommend it enough to visit Venice in the winter. When it's not crowded, the piazze take on an extra loveliness, especially during the end-of-year holidays.

For transportation, walk or take the water taxi (*vaporetto*). Gondolas, of course, are Venetian icons, but a ride is expensive enough that they're best used for the experience rather than as a means to get from Point A to Point B.

Apartments or hotels in Cannaregio or Castello are your best bet for getting around quickly.

Kid-Friendly Things to Do:

- Trying *Cicchetti*: These small bites, the Venetian equivalent of Spanish tapas, are kid-friendly and easy to eat. Little ones open to trying new foods will appreciate cicchetti dishes. Plus, there won't be any food stains to worry about!

Activities for Any Age:

- Explore Doge's Palace Prisons: Skip the line by booking a guided tour to see the Doge's Palace prisons in the heart of downtown Venice. (The tour costs around 56€ per person.)
- Mask-Making Class: Your family can share the experience of crafting your own iconic carnival masks as you learn hands-on about this ancient Venetian art form. (Prices start from 55€ per person).
- Glass-Blowing Demonstration: Head to the island of Murano to see this craft in action, and even pick out a small ornament to bring home! (Contact Ellegi Murano Glass directly to find out more).

Emilia-Romagna

Emilia-Romagna has a little bit to suit all tastes. Kids will love the city's race cars, colorful mosaics, and mouthwatering food; you're in for a treat!

Many of this region's larger cities are stroller-friendly, and you'll appreciate their green spaces, too.

I recommend avoiding this part of the country if you want to visit in the summer and see primarily urban areas. Developed areas of this region can get way too hot to have fun in. Spring and fall, however, have the best weather and much smaller crowds.

Major cities like Bologna can be easily accessed by train and local buses; otherwise, it's a good idea to have a car so you can explore on your own.

While hotels or apartments in either Modena, Bologna, or Ravenna will undoubtedly fit the bill, opting for a farm (agriturismo) accommodation in the countryside will allow for a completely absorbing experience.

Activities for Any Age:

- Visit Race Car Museums: Emilia-Romagna's motor valley houses the headquarters of Ferrari, Lamborghini, and Maserati. Car enthusiasts in your family will never forget visiting the homes of these iconic brands!
- Mason's Labyrinth: Everyone will love exploring this gigantic 8-hectare bamboo labyrinth and checking out what was once Franco Maria Ricci's collection of illustrious typography and graphics.
- Go Shopping: Hit the high street in Emilia-Romagna and bond with your teen over some much-needed retail therapy. I recommend trying Fidenza Village.

Cinque Terre

A trip to Cinque Terre is best enjoyed when you have the freedom of hiking without a stroller or your baby's sleep schedule in mind. Strollers are viable in villages and on the path from Riomaggiore to Manarola (known as the Street of Love (Via dell'Amore)), but if you come with a baby, it's best to bring a carrier just in case.

This area is ideal for being active. Whether swimming, boating, or hiking, sport-loving families will enjoy all that the five villages —Monterosso al Mare, Vernazza, Corniglia, Manarola, and Riomaggiore—have to offer. Spring and fall have the best weather and fewer crowds, but it can still be rainy. Summer, of course, has the best weather, but it's jam-packed.

There's no need for a car here. In fact, driving is not allowed in any of the towns, making the shoe-polished street lanes incredibly safe and family-friendly. Walk between the villages and other area trails, or take the local train.

Reserve a hotel or apartment in one of the five villages. This will allow you to stay "in the action" by easily exploring the other villages in the morning or evening.

Activities for Any Age:

- Hike the Renowned Trails: Explore Cinque Terre's most beloved activity by taking the main coastal hiking route—the Blue Path (Sentiero Azzurro)—which connects the five villages. This allows for convenient travel and offers the perfect way to sightsee while staying active.
- Discover the Beaches of Monterosso: Immerse yourself in the pristine waters of Monterosso's beaches, especially favoring the quieter ones situated on the "old town side." For a full day of relaxation, I suggest Tragaglia Beach as an ideal spot to unwind and soak up the sun.

- Experience the Picturesque Train Journeys Between Towns: The train system serves as the primary mode of transportation within Cinque Terre, attracting many travelers seeking a scenic adventure. Embark on the Cinque Terre Express, a delightful journey connecting each village from La Spezia to Levanto. Teens, in particular, will relish this preview of their future travels.

Lake Garda

Resting in Northern Italy, Lake Garda might not offer that Mediterranean *Mamma Mia* feeling, but its nonetheless stunning natural scenery will undoubtedly take your family's breath away.

With 12 theme parks (operating year-round) to choose from, adrenaline junkies in your family will be kept very busy, while nature lovers will enjoy the glittering lake waters nearby.

Traveling by car is possible, but traffic can be congested, so I encourage you to grab ferries on the lake instead. More than just being practical, this mode of transportation is a unique way to soak in all the fabulous views to be found. Also, depending on where you're staying, you can walk to your destinations.

Book a family-friendly apartment or bungalow in Garda Shore (Riva del Garda) or a campsite in Garda Fishery (Peschiera del Garda).

Kid-Friendly Things to Do:

- Theme Parks: Here are some theme parks in the Lake Garda area that your kids won't stop talking about: Gardaland Resort, CanevaWorld Resort, Gardaland Sea Life Aquarium, LEGOLAND Water Park, Caneva Aquapark, Movieland, Medieval Times, Busatte Adventure Park, Natura Viva Park, Parco Giardino Sigurtà Nature Park, Elias Adventure Park, and Jungle Adventure Park. They're just as popular with Italians as they are with visitors!
- Sirmione's Castle: Climb the Scaligero Castle of Sirmione (Castello Scaligero di Sirmione). This fortress was fully functional in the 14th century and is now one of the country's best-preserved structures. Walk along the fort's walls and climb the tower for an incredible bird's-eye view of the city.

DOING IT YOUR WAY...

Travelers braving their first lone getaway will hopefully be at ease now that we've covered some key points about journeying solo. Members of the LGBTQIA+ community can rest easy now that they know some of the most inclusive places to visit. Likewise, parents who had previously panicked over how to plan the perfect itinerary (with a bit of luck) can now rest assured that their trip will be one over which the family will reminisce for years to come. Whatever your situation, bike, hike, or drive it your way!

As we near the end of this humble guide, couples, now it's your turn to get recommendations on how to craft your most romantic getaway yet.

CHAPTER 7
COUPLE'S GETAWAY

 Scusami, but you see, back in old Napoli, that's *amore!*

(BROOKS & WARREN, 1953)

O r so the 1950s Dean Martin classic goes in its timeless tribute to the highest of our human emotions. Perhaps it's just the whiff of strong espresso pervading the streets or even the gentle splashing of corner street fountains. Yet, it seems that even the most minor things in Italy, which we might take for granted anywhere else, somehow become more romantic here. No wonder it is known as a nation of amore (love)!

Whisking your significant other off on any getaway abroad is lovely, but making your destination one of the world's most spellbinding may bring you closer than anywhere else ever could. The country is filled with magic (*see Chapters 3 and 5*), so there's no need to worry about picking a place to wow your partner. Still, you might want to decide which out-of-the-ordinary activities you'd like to experience together and then go from there. This chapter will help you craft your perfect romantic escape!

Before we begin, here's something to consider: For your itinerary, try to balance your time out and about with breaks for some relaxing downtime where you can reconnect. In Bella Italia, beauty is around every corner, so, if possible, choose the types of places and experiences that you and your partner love most. But then again, having a few romantic surprises hidden up your sleeve is not a bad idea either! My advice: Stay present and enjoy your little moments together rather than trying to fit in every popular site just because. This jewel of the Mediterranean has stood the test of time and will wait eagerly for you and your partner to return for more.

LOVE KNOWS NO BOUNDS

Are you and your partner in the mood for love? Amore will be in the air as you escape together to some of Italy's perfect places for couples. Don't worry if your heart skips a beat – it just means you've caught the magic! Basking in the sunset, strolling together under the stars, exploring the vast cities, or gazing out at the rolling hills, you and your love will make memories to last a lifetime in these, the Bel Paese's most romantic locales:

Venice

Float away on one of the world's sleekest crafts. Take a gondola ride through the city's waterways–an excursion on which your cheerful gondolier will most likely serenade you and your partner!

Verona

Fair Verona is sure to enchant even the most pragmatic couples. Make sweeping declarations of love under the fabled Gothic-style stone balcony at Juliet's House (Casa di Giulietta) on Cappello Street (Via Cappello), which is said to have inspired Shakespeare's *Romeo and Juliet* (1997).

Florence

The "Cradle of the Renaissance" has held on to so many influences and cultures that it might seem only natural to return the favor. Why not lock in your love on the railings of the Old Bridge (Ponte Vecchio) as you take in its long-standing history? (*See Chapter 5 for more on Ponte Vecchio and Florence*).

The 463-step climb up the Cathedral of St. Mary of the Flower (Cattedrale di Santa Maria del Fiore) is a breeze when shared with your love, especially with the magnificent frescoes you'll see before you gaze upon the stunning city views together at the top.

Rome

I recommend booking a Roman Holiday for honeymoons, anniversaries, and spontaneous getaways–all Vespas included. The capital is, without a doubt, one of the peninsula's most captivating fairytales. Flick a coin in the city's Baroque-style stoned Trevi fountain for good luck.

Palermo

However small, the vibrant island of Sicily has retained its influence as a cultural crossroads that once linked the legendary Arab and Byzantine empires through its Mediterranean trade routes.

Sicily's majestic Pilgrim Mountain (Monte Pellegrino) stands at the east bay of the island's capital, Palermo. The two-to-three-hour climb will have you and your partner losing yourselves in each other's company amid the breathtaking panoramas. At the top, you'll be excited to re-enter civilization at a small square where you can sit and enjoy a well-deserved coffee together.

Milan

Fall in love all over again in Milan's charming district of Brera, where your evening stroll (*passeggiata*) will be dotted with twinkling fairy lights draped overhead. Down the narrow alleys of Brera's old town neighborhood, you can browse the knickknacks and keepsakes at Bright Flower Street's (Via Fiori Chiari's) flea market on the third Sunday of every month except August.

Turin

You will have the entire city of Turin at your feet as you take your love to new heights on Superga Mountain (Monte Superga). The metropolis lights up at night, offering views of Vittorio Square (Piazza Vittorio), the Po River, and the Alps.

Indulge your sweet tooth by sharing the city's creation—*gianduiotto* chocolate—named after Gianduja, a traditional Piedmontese carnival character.

Trapani

Trapani is a lovers' paradise with its serene harbor nestled peacefully at the foot of the waves. Stroll down the coastline with your beloved and make your way to the city's main park, Villa Margherita, for sweeping sea views. Then, take a cable car (*funivia*) from there to the lovely nearby town of Erice, where you can stroll through the cobblestone streets, visit the Castle of Venus (Castello di Venere), and enjoy time and more scenic views together in the Balio Garden (Giardino del Balio).

Bellagio

Bellagio is one of Lake Como's most romantic havens. Gorgeous land-scaped gardens are peppered all around town, and you'll also find incredible views over the water and the snow-capped mountains. These natural delights will accompany you and your partner as you scale up the narrow streets leading to the city's most famous view-point at the top of Salita Serbelloni Street (Via Salita Serbelloni). For a quieter, still romantic time together, consider the nearby fishing village of Pescallo.

OUT IN THE WILD

Italy is a veritable paradise for couples who crave outdoor fun. Featuring gorgeous mountain peaks, challenging hiking and biking trails, and almost 1,500 lakes, there are activities in nature to suit everyone's tastes.

Without further ado, here are my recommendations for the romantic *and* adventurous:

Trebbia Valley

Uncork the essence of the Trebbia Valley with a bottle of bubbly as you discover the northern region's tucked-away mountain escape. Don't miss your chance to watch (and maybe even participate in) Trebbia's grape harvest—email the Bonelli winery (Cantine Bonelli) for details.

Lake Garda

Get your adrenaline pumping by challenging each other during a multisport week in Lake Garda. Bike your way to glacial lakes, hike to new heights on the Iron Path (Via Ferrata), and explore mesmerizing river gorges. Save yourself the stress by organizing your itinerary, equipment, and accommodation for your adventure through a local guide. Contact Dolomite Mountains online for more information.

Amalfi Coast

Romance will soak the very earth under your feet as you tread together in sacred footsteps on the Amalfi Coast's 5.9-mile (9.5-km) point-to-point "Path of the Gods" (Sentiero degli Dei). The trail gets its name from Homer's epic poem, *The Odyssey*, which tells that the Greek Gods fashioned this hallowed ground in an attempt to save the main hero, Ulysses, from a lethal band of sirens on the islands of Li Galli.

Cinque Terre

There are over 74.5 miles (119.9 km) of coastline along the five towns of Cinque Terre, and all of it is waiting to be discovered. The cliffside beauty of Cinque Terre is the perfect destination for couples crazy about hiking; there are just under 50 routes you can choose from for your next escapade together!

Courmayeur

Skiing is first class in Mont Blanc during the wintertime. Always under the watchful eyes of a local guide, feed your need for speed on many of the intermediate ski paths (*pistes*) along the back of the Alps, or consider going off-piste for a slower descent. Even if skiing isn't what gets your blood flowing, consider taking the Helbronner cable car up the side of Mont Blanc for unforgettable views.

SEASIDE SERENITY

The mellow climate surrounds you as you dig your toes in a powdery white-sand beach. Overlooking the ocean, the horizon stretches before you as far as the eye can see. With dusk approaching, the sun is finally swallowed whole by the vast and gentle waves lapping at the shoreline.

Experience sunset magic by the sea like no other during your romantic wanderings (*for insights into specific beach destinations, flip back to Chapter 3 for inspiration*). Here are my top picks for coastal

bliss—destinations and activities guaranteed to foster deeper connections between you and your partner against an effervescent seaside
backdrop.

Capri

Look out for the dolphins gliding past the ferries leaving from Naples,
Sorrento, or Positano to the enchanting island of Capri. Your hearts
will beat easily for Capri's dazzling beauty, fragrant subtropical vege-
tation, and year-round balminess.

Chart the Bay of Naples privately or on a guided boat tour to explore
the Phlegraean Islands—Ischia, Procida, Vivara, and Nisida. Each one
is fabulous for a day trip in the sun!

Delight in the surroundings of the Blue Grotto (Grotta Azzura),
which completely transforms in the noonday sun. Be sure to duck
your heads when sliding into the nifty cave opening. As the rays
pierce the water, dyeing it a liquid sapphire, marvel at the white sandy
seabed below, which seems to gleam like silver.

The cave itself is 177 feet (54 m) long, 49 feet (14.9 m) high, and 98
feet (29.9 m) wide and is said to have formed into a kind of
nymphaeum—a shrine dedicated to nymphs. From this one, Emperor
Tiberius ruled over Rome in the 1st century.

Cinque Terre

Romance is also the order of the day (and night) in Cinque Terre,
which you and your partner may feel were tailor-made for couples.
You'll both love walking on the beaches as your eyes dart between the
blue waters and colorful buildings high above. Then, after a magical
day, enjoy the local lemony liqueur—*limoncino* (limoncello's close
cousin)—together at dinner as you bask in the glow of a timeless
Italian sunset!

Taormina

Resurrect the fleeting essence of the sweet life (*la dolce vita*) beyond the silver screen of the 1960s by including the picturesque east coast town of Taormina, Sicily, on your Italian itinerary. Explore the depths below this corner of the island by booking an unforgettable snorkeling or scuba diving trip. I recommend the Taormina Diving Center or the Blue Sea Diving Center for either activity.

Portofino

Indulge in a slice of the Italian Riviera by doing nothing all day except hopping from one of Portofino's terraced cafés to the next. Stroll hand in hand along the waterfront promenade or climb up to Brown Castle (Castello Brown) for breathtaking views of the town and sea.

Positano

The cliffside village of Positano spills off the Amalfi Coast in a cascade of white-washed cottages flecked with garden greenery. This once sleepy little fishing village has grown very popular, but it is still a perfect romantic getaway. Enjoy an evening walk along Big Beach (Spiaggia Grande), followed by a gorgeous sunset boat ride in the blue-green waters of the Mediterranean.

A 4.4-mile (7-km) trip to the celebrated Emerald Grotto (Grotta dello Smeraldo) is best done at noontime. Huddled in the rowboat, the cave will seem to have transported you both to another world as the midday sun illuminates the water, tinging the stalactites and stony walls in a pale pastel green.

Tuscany

The unique geography of the Bel Paese makes for close connections between the land and sea along its coastal outline. Think undulating hills, slender cypress trees, and babbling hot springs, and you've captured the popular image of Tuscany. People often forget that this region has a coast–and a long one at that. Running all the way from sunny southern Orbetello to the beaches strung along the edge of the

Apuan Alps, the Tuscan coast makes up over 130 miles (209 km) of Italian shoreline.

Choose some days when the weather and winds help push more surf-worthy swells in from the sea, and you'll find the coastlines of Piombino and Livorno offer surfers the chance to ride some outstanding waves. This is a fantastic way of basking in the country's natural beauty with your love.

Lake Districts

In the Lake Districts of Como and Garda, you and your partner can hitch up to a motorboat for an afternoon of waterskiing at its finest.

Thanks to the consistency of its main winds, Ora and Pelèr, Lake Garda is also considered one of the best destinations in Europe for windsurfers of all levels.

Ostuni

Located just 3.1 miles (5 km) from the dazzling coast, Ostuni is the perfect destination for couples looking to strike a nice balance between land and sea.

TABLE FOR TWO

The quickest way to almost all hearts is through the stomach, and I'm glad to say that when it comes to the perfect dinner date, Bella Italia is more than willing to serve up its finest. Share the culinary magic of Italian cuisine, which varies from coast to coast. Foodie (*buongustaio*) couples, read on. This final section of the chapter will go over each region's culinary specialty to highlight some of the country's most romantic restaurants and delicious food tours.

Venice

- **Harry's Bar**

Venice's iconic Harry's Bar began in 1931 when bartender Giuseppe Cipriani (inventor of the signature Italian cocktail "the Bellini" and the *carpaccio* beef dish) decided to name his establishment after Harry Pickering, a long-time patron of the Hotel Europa bar. There's enough celebrity panache here to inspire a visit from any couple.

- **DOCG's Prosecco Superiore**

While many people enjoy a glass of store-bought Prosecco, far fewer can say that they've visited the Prosecco vineyards of Italy in the flesh. Located just an hour from the Floating City of Venice in a small region between Conegliano and Valdobbiadene in Veneto, you and your partner can discover the highest quality Italian wine classification: DOCG. The evermore stringent Prosecco Superiore DOCG regulations mean that your glass is 100% premium, right down to the last bubble.

On a Prosecco tour (or even just you and your partner), you'll find that most of these wineries welcome guests with open arms as they happily show off their vineyards and facilities and, perhaps, even give you a taste!

- **Rialto Market**

Live life like a true local by shopping at the Rialto Market, Venice's oldest. Named after its settlement on the high bank (Rivo Alto), the busyness of Rialto hasn't changed much from antiquity, when merchants unloaded spices and foods from the East. Today, you can purchase similarly tasty treasures, from seasonal fruits to fresh cheeses.

Puglia

• Friselle at Osteria Monacelle

Sink your teeth into the region's specialty, *friselle*, at Ostuni's Osteria Monacelle. Made with toasted bread, friselle were once the practical lunches of farmers and fishermen whose hard days of physical labor or long journeys at sea required maximum nutrition that kept well. Chefs Melina and her daughter Francesca use Tumminia wheat (a type of durum wheat grown in western Sicily) for their version of these twice-baked rolls, which are sliced, dried in the oven until they crust over to a crunchy hardness, and then topped with cherry tomatoes, oregano, and olive oil.

• Olive Oil Tasting Tour

Amble among ancient olive trees while you and your love visit local oil mills on an oil-tasting tour in Ostuni.

Turin

• Nonna Cleme

Make a reservation at this family-run pizzeria, which is also perfect for a fun date night. As hinted in its name, Nonna Cleme rustles up grandma's classic pizza recipes in many varieties, and they are simply delicious. Be sure to check out Nonna's vegan, vegetarian, and gluten-free options, too!

• Chocolate Tour

"Go nuts" for the popular flavor combination of chocolate with hazelnut in the City of Chocolate, home to the decadent chocolate-y, hazelnut-ty spread beloved by foodies worldwide. Limits on Turin's procurement of cocoa during the Napoleonic Wars led to the invention of Giandula, a blend of chocolate with a delicate 30% hazelnut paste. Indulge yourselves in a sugar rush on a chocolate-themed tour of the city!

Milan

- ## Osteria del Treno

If you recently saw Stanley Tucci *Searching for Italy* around Milan, the celeb stopped at this traditional osteria for a quick bite of jaw-dropping *osso buco* (veal shank and potatoes) (CNN, 2021). Osteria del Treno has been serving this and other slow-cooked foods like saffron-dusted risotto for years. The restaurant's Sala Liberty ballroom was built in 1898 as a union hall for Milan rail workers who worked at the nearby Stazione Centrale (central station).

Sicily

- ## Otto Geleng

Savor Sicilian *"gastronomia"* like no other at executive chef Roberto Toro's Baroque-inspired restaurant, Otto Geleng, in coastal Taormina. Clink your crystal glasses while overlooking the sweeping landscapes of Mount Etna and the Ionian Sea at this Michelin-starred eatery (Michelin, 2024).

- ## Montelepre's Sfincia di Priescia Food Festival

Every 6th of January, Sicilian residents welcome this festival (*sagra*) to celebrate (and devour lots of) their traditional treat, *sfinica di priescia*. Partake in this sweet festivity at Prince of Piedmont Square (Piazza Principe di Piemonte) to share the locals' love of their deep-fried pretzel-shaped pastry (not to be confused with *churros*!).

- **Ballarò Market**

East of Montelepre, you'll discover Palermo's largest and oldest market, Ballarò. Here, you'll brush shoulders with locals as you bargain with vendors over meats, cheeses, and fish. Wedged between rows of market stands, there is also a lively weekly flea market where you can search for treasures to take home.

Bologna

- **Sfoglia Rina**

Of all the delectable restaurant options in Bologna, English celebrity chef Rick Stein sat down to dinner at humble Sfoglia Rina (BBC, 2016). Dubbed "pasta heaven" since Grandma Rina opened it as a pasta shop in 1963, this unique eatery is somewhat of a pasta laboratory; its team of on-site chefs continues to push the boundaries of the classic carbohydrate's versatility (BBC, 2016).

- **Bologna Food Tour**

Eating your way through the Bel Paese is a task so ambitious that it has caused many to suffer major food comas. Avoid indigestion by letting the experts take the reins as you and your partner experience iconic Emilia-Romagna fare like prosciutto, balsamic vinegar, and Parmigiano Reggiano cheeses from Bologna to Modena.

- **Quadrilatero**

Adjacent to the Main Square (Piazza Maggiore), Bologna's nourishing market provides more than just food for the spirit. It dates back centuries and was once filled with medieval guilds of fishmongers, butchers, bakers, and goldsmith artisans. At the Quadrilatero of today, enjoy a light drink and snack (*aperitivo*) before a delicious dinner.

Naples

- **Pizzaria La Notizia**

Renowned as *"the* place for excellent pizza," according to the Michelin guide, La Notizia throws together fresh ingredients and bakes them perfectly in the oven, so let's eat (*mangiamo!*) (Michelin, 2024). Self-professed pizza chef (*pizzaiolo*) "with an identity, a brain, and a soul," Enzo Coccia, grounds this pizzeria's culinary identity in the vividness of Naples, where visitors looking for the signature sourdough dish will find nothing short of a palatable masterpiece (Coccia, n.d.).

- **La Pignasecca Market**

The La Pignasecca market might be small compared to others in the city, but few can rival this hub's vitality and affordable produce. This is where you go to eat like a local.

Rome

- **Armando al Pantheon**

Since 1961, Armando al Pantheon has been dishing out hearty meals in its cozy atmosphere, combining its culinary identity with typical Roman cuisine. Just be sure to make a reservation—there is only seating for 20!

- **Imàgo**

For a truly unforgettable dining experience, look no further than the Michelin-starred eatery Imàgo, located close to the Spanish Steps on the sixth floor of the Hassler Hotel. Here, you can enjoy dishes that test the boundaries of texture and flavor (Michelin, 2024) while taking in amazing views of the Eternal City together.

- **Pasta-Making Class**

Plunge your arms elbow-deep in flour for the complete Roman experience at a pasta-making class. The best classes include a lesson from an expert Italian chef and, of course, a taste of an excellent wine (*vino*).

Tuscany

- **Ristorante Buca Lapi**

Nestled on Trebbio Street (Via del Trebbio), Florence's Buca Lapi creates magic underground in the basements of Renaissance-era Antinori Palace (Palazzo Antinori), which belonged to the Antinori family over 100 years ago. The Antinoris of that time decided to open a restaurant (*ristorante*) and hired Orazio Lapi as the tavern keeper, who kept stock of the wine in the cellar, known as a *buca* (hole). This humble server impressed the family so much that the restaurant was dedicated in his honor, and it has been a favorite among locals, celebrities, and royals alike ever since. It is said that even the glamorous Grace Kelly thoroughly enjoyed her meal here back in the '60s. So, don your best outfit and toast your love at Tuscany's finest Florentine fairytale.

- **Truffle Hunting**

One of Italy's most exquisite (and expensive) foods is the mighty truffle, and any foodie couple will love going on a hunt around rural Tuscany for these mushrooms. Go on the adventure together to learn what it takes to be a truffle connoisseur using trained sniffer dogs.

THAT'S AMORE

Lose yourselves in an Italian fairytale. I hope this chapter has offered some inspiring ideas for your romantic getaway, from the day's activities to the evening's dinner under the stars. Remember to savor each moment. After all, that's *amore* (love)!

KEEPING THE GAME ALIVE

Now that you have everything you need to travel safer, discover hidden Italian gems, learn the lingo, and experience the real Italy, I would be so grateful if you would pass on your newfound knowledge and show other readers where they can find the same help.

Simply by leaving your honest opinion of this book on Amazon, you'll show other solo adventurers, LGBTQIA+ travelers, women, families, and couples where they can find the information they're looking for and share your passion for travel to Italy.

Thank you for your help. Safe travel and authentic experiences in Italy are kept alive when we tell others about what we've learned – and you're helping me to do just that.

Scan the QR code to leave your review on Amazon.

CONCLUSION

The studio apartment was just how I left it—messy. I guess I was half expecting the world I'd left behind to have changed as much as I had after my first time in the Bel Paese.

The mundaneness of my old life set against the recent liveliness of Italy was the straw that (blessedly) broke the camel's back. As I came down from the highs of travel, I decided then and there, standing in the middle of my place, that I would pack up and leave for Bella Italia. Permanently. I would extend for the foreseeable future what was originally only supposed to be a brief European getaway to get over my ex. Couldn't life, I pondered, be one big adventure?

And so, there you have it–this travel guide is one of the many fruits of my Italian adventures. I hope it's been valuable for you. *If it has helped your trip in any way, I would be so grateful if you would leave a review.*

The best way to take these writings is to use them as a springboard from which you might dive further into those destinations beyond these pages–some of which have escaped my memory and experience.

Be brave; say "yes" to what you might have refused if you were anywhere else, like in your home city. Isn't that what travel is about—

being a bit bold, taking chances, and having new experiences? After all, we all have our own stories to write.

I wish you safe travels. Be well...

REFERENCES

ABC News. (2024). *New requirements coming in 2024 for Americans traveling to Europe.* Retrieved from https://abcnews.go.com/GMA/Travel/new-requirements-coming-2024-americans-traveling-europe/story?id=101546203

Aelums. (2021, June 23). *Solo traveling in Italy as a woman.* Retrieved from https://www.reddit.com/r/solotravel/comments/o6czw2/solo_travelling_in_italy_as_a_woman/?share_id=XBE04m0FoD5YS1HrBVIWE

Alighieri, D. (2003). *Inferno* (J. Ciardi, Trans.). New American Library.

Alison Chino. (n.d.). *Riomaggiore, Italy.* Retrieved from https://www.alisonchino.com/riomaggiore-italy/

American Express. (n.d.). *Should you pay in local or home currency when traveling?* Retrieved from https://www.americanexpress.com/en-us/credit-cards/credit-intel/should-you-pay-in-local-or-home-currency-when-traveling/

Anile, Alberto. (2013). *Orson Welles in Italy.* Indiana University Press.

Ask a Manager. (2017, July). *European clients are sneering at my American colleagues' table manners.* Retrieved from https://www.askamanager.org/2017/07/european-clients-are-sneering-at-my-american-colleagues-table-manners.html

Australian Government. (n.d.). *Italy travel advice & safety.* Smartraveller. Retrieved from https://www.smartraveller.gov.au/destinations/europe/italy

Avventure Bellissime. (2023). *Off the beaten path in Italy: 10 spots you can't miss!* Retrieved from https://www.tours-italy.com/blog/secret-italy-north-south-10-beaten-path-spots-you-cant-miss-1

Basil & Grape. (n.d.). *The best wine for Italian food.* Retrieved from https://www.basilandgrape.com/the-best-wine-for-italian-food/

BBC. (2016, May 20). Bologna (Season 1, Episode 5) [TV series episode]. In R. Stein's Long Weekends.

Benvenuto Limos. (n.d.). *Interesting facts: Galleria Vittorio Emanuele II, Milan – world's oldest shopping mall.* Retrieved from https://www.benvenutolimos.com/blog/interesting-facts-galleria-vittorio-emanuele-ii-milan-worlds-oldest-shopping-mall/

Be Prepared. (n.d.). *5 ways to prepare for disasters while you travel.* Retrieved from https://www.beprepared.com/blogs/articles/5-ways-to-prepare-for-disasters-while-you-travel

Berlitz Country Guide (1988/1989). A Macmillan Company.

Blue Sea Diving. (n.d.). *Blue Sea Diving Center Taormina.* Retrieved from https://blueseadiving.it/

Bologna Welcome. (n.d.). *Bologna: LGBTI friendly.* Retrieved from https://www.bolognawelcome.com/en/blog/bologna-lgbti-friendly-en

Brepols. (n.d.). Retrieved from https://www.brepols.net/products/IS-9781912554683-1

Broccoli, B. (Producer), & Fukunaga, C. (Director). (2021). *No time to die* [Film]. Metro-Goldwyn-Mayer.

Brooks, H., & Warren, J. (1953). That's amore [Recorded by Dean Martin]. On *Dean Martin: The Capitol years* [Album]. Capitol Records. https://genius.com/Dean-martin-thats-amore-lyrics

Burton, R. F. (Trans.). (1885). *The book of the thousand nights and a night* (Vol. 6). Burton Club.

Care Health Insurance. (n.d.) *5 essentials your travel insurance plan should cover.* (n.d.). Retrieved from https://www.careinsurance.com/blog/travel-insurance-articles/5-essential-covers-to-check-in-your-travel-insurance-plan

Celebrity Cruises. (n.d.). *Best food cities in Italy.* Retrieved from https://www.celebrity cruises.com/blog/best-food-cities-in-italy

Champion Traveler. (n.d.). *Cost of a trip to Italy & the cheapest time to visit Italy.* Retrieved from https://championtraveler.com/price/cost-of-a-trip-to-italy/

Cimbaitaly. (n.d.). *Cinque Terre: Favorite place in Italy.* Retrieved from https://cimbaitaly.com/blog/katie/cinque-terre-favorite-place-italy/

Citalia. (n.d.). *Ravello festival.* Retrieved from https://www.citalia.com/holidays/italy/campania/amalfi-coast/ravello/ravello-festival/

City Wonders. (n.d.). *Italian phrases for travelers with pronunciation.* Retrieved from https://citywonders.com/blog/Italy/Rome/italian-pronunciation-guide-key-phrases

Clarke, A., & Castleman, M. (Eds.). (2006). Survival Italian in *Frommer's Italian Phrasebook and Culture Guide* (pp. 1-39). Wiley Publishing. Retrieved from https://catalogimages.wiley.com/images/db/pdf/0471793019.excerpt.pdf

CNN. (2021, March 7). Milan (Season 1, Episode 4) [TV series episode]. In S. Tucci (Host), Stanley Tucci: Searching for Italy. CNN. Available on Prime Video, CNN, discovery+, Hulu, Sling TV, Max.

Coccia, E. (n.d.). *About Enzo Coccia.* Retrieved from http://www.enzococcia.com/en/about-enzo-coccia/

Commisceo Global. (2019). *Italy - language, culture, customs and etiquette.* Retrieved from www.Commisceo-Global.com

Condé Nast Traveler. (2018, February 8). *The 10 best hidden beaches in Italy.* Retrieved from https://www.cntraveler.com/gallery/best-hidden-beaches-in-italy

Cope, Marie Anne. (2013). *Try not to lose your head.* Retrieved from https://www.marieannecope.com/blog/try-not-to-lose-your-head/

Course Hero. (n.d.). *Italian nationalism.* Retrieved from https://www.coursehero.com/file/80405230/Italian-Nationalism-Docspdf/

Criscione, C. (2023, April 16). *Best places to visit in Italy with kids - by a mom in Italy.* Mom in Italy. Retrieved from https://mominitaly.com/best-places-to-visit-in-italy-with-kids/

The Culture Trip. (n.d.). *From taboo to mainstream: How Milan's LGBTQ+ community found itself through music.* Retrieved from https://theculturetrip.com/europe/italy/articles/from-taboo-to-mainstream-how-milans-lgbtq-community-found-itself-through-music

Curata Travel. (n.d.). *Tips for booking your flights to Italy.* Retrieved from https://curata travel.com/blogs/curata-travel-blog/tips-for-booking-your-flights-to-italy

Dalla, L. (1972). Piazza grande [Song]. On *Storie di casa mia* [Album]. RCA Italiana.

Di Capua, E., & Mazzucchi, G. (1898). 'O sole mio.

D2 Detours. (n.d.). *Italy to Hungary: A quickish exit from the Schengen zone.* Retrieved from https://d2detours.com/italy-to-hungary-a-quickish-exit-from-the-schengen-zone/

EDiplomat. (2016). *Cultural etiquette: Italy.* Retrieved from http://www.ediplomat.com/ np/cultural_etiquette/ce_it.htm

Etiquette Scholar; Yellowstone Publishing, LLC. (2019). *Italy dining etiquette.* Retrieved from https://www.etiquettescholar.com/dining_etiquette/table-etiquette/europe-m_table_manners/italian_dining_etiquette.html

Europass. (2017). *Europass.* Retrieved from https://europass.europa.eu/en

Evason, N. (2017). *Italian culture - etiquette.* Cultural Atlas. Retrieved from https://cultur alatlas.sbs.com.au/italian-culture/italian-culture-etiquette

Expedia. (n.d.). *Province of Catanzaro.* Retrieved from https://www.expedia. co.uk/Province-Of-Catanzaro.dx6051439

Explore. (n.d.). *Visit Europe's largest waterfront square: Trieste, Friuli Venezia Giulia, Italy.* Retrieved from https://www.explore.com/1390024/visit-europes-largest-water front-square-trieste-friuli-venezia-giulia-italy/

Festitalia. (n.d.). *Italian heritage month: Culinary.* Retrieved from https://www.festitalia. ca/italian-heritage-month-culinary/

Fayed, A. (2024). *15 dos and don't of eating in Italy part 2 – eating in Italy.* Generate Press. Retrieved from https://expats.adamfayed.com/15-dos-and-dont-of-eating-in-italy-part-2-eating-in-italy/

Fearlessly Italy. (2023). *15 famous museums in Italy to include in your itinerary.* Retrieved from https://fearlesslyitaly.com/famous-museums-in-italy/

Ferrante, E. (2018). *My brilliant friend. Book 1, the Neapolitan novels.* The Text Publishing Company.

FIA Region I. (n.d.). *European road safety charter.* Retrieved from https://www.fiaregion1. com/european-road-safety-charter/

Fodor's Travel. (n.d.). *Venice in January.* Retrieved from https://www.fodors.com/ community/europe/venice-in-jan-999487/

Forums Well Trained Mind. (n.d.). *People in the United States: Do you wait until everyone is served before you begin eating?* Retrieved from https://forums.welltrainedmind.com/ topic/528423-people-in-the-united-states-do-you-wait-until-everyone-is-served-before-you-begin-eating/page/2/

Frankovich, S., & Wyler, W. (Producers), & Wyler, W. (Director). (1953). *Roman holiday* [Film]. Paramount Pictures.

Gamintraveler. (2024, April 5). *7 best places to visit in Italy with kids.* Retrieved from https://www.gamintraveler.com/2024/03/23/best-places-to-visit-in-italy/

Get Your Guide. (n.d.). *Ostuni olive oil tasting tour.* Retrieved from https://www.getyour guide.com/ostuni-l2729/ostuni-olive-oil-tasting-tour-t400388/

Giartosio, T., & Goretti, G. (2006). *La città e l'isola.* Donzelli Editore.

The Glittering Unknown. (n.d.). *Cinque Terre: Riomaggiore to Manarola*. Retrieved from https://www.theglitteringunknown.com/cinque-terre-riomaggiore-manarola/

Global Peace Index Map. (2023). *Vision of humanity*. Institute for Economics and Peace (IEP). Retrieved from https://www.visionofhumanity.org/resources/global-peace-index-2023/

Google Sites. (n.d.) *A new threat: Part I Italian dubbed*. Retrieved from https://sites.google.com/view/7terpratincpa

Gov.uk. (n.d.). *EU, EEA and Swiss citizens*. Retrieved from https://www.gov.uk/eu-eea

Gov.uk. (n.d.). *Foreign travel advice: Italy*. Retrieved from https://www.gov.uk/foreign-travel-advice/italy

Gov.uk. (n.d.). *Foreign travel advice: Italy – safety and security*. Retrieved from https://www.gov.uk/foreign-travel-advice/italy/safety-and-security

Goodreads. (n.d.). *Elena Ferrante quotes*. Retrieved from https://www.goodreads.com/author/quotes/44085.Elena_Ferrante

Goodreads. (n.d.). *If you don't try, nothing ever changes*. Retrieved from https://www.goodreads.com/quotes/8041750-if-you-don-t-try-nothing-ever-changes

GRIAA. (2014). *PapSpring 2014*. Retrieved from https://www.griaa.org/wp-content/uploads/2014/04/GRIAA_PapSpring-2014.pdf

Hidden Italy. (n.d.). *Useful hints before traveling*. Retrieved from https://www.hiddenitaly.com/regional-information/useful-hints-before-traveling/

HI USA. (n.d.). *How to keep a travel journal*. Retrieved from https://www.hiusa.org/blog/travel-hacks-tips/how-to-keep-a-travel-journal

History Place. (n.d.). *Garibaldi's speech*. Retrieved from https://www.historyplace.com/speeches/garibaldi.htm

Homer. (1996). *The odyssey* (R. Fagles, Trans.). Penguin Books. (Original work published ca. 8th century BCE)

ILGA. (2019). *The International Lesbian, Gay, Bisexual, Trans and Intersex Association*. Retrieved from https://ilga.org/

Instantly Italy. (n.d.). *All saints day in Italy*. Retrieved from https://instantlyitaly.com/all-saints-day-in-italy/

International Lesbian, Gay, Bisexual, Trans and Intersex Association. (2019, December). *ILGA world map: Sexual orientation laws*. Retrieved from https://ilga.org/downloads/ILGA_World_map_sexual_orientation_laws_December2019.pdf

Istituto Nazionale di Statistica (I.Stat.). (2024) *Resident population on 1 January*. http://dati.istat.it/Index.aspx?QueryId=18460

IT - Trenitalia. (n.d.). Retrieved from www.trenitalia.com

Italia Like a Local. (n.d.). *How to plan a trip to Italy*. Retrieved from https://www.italialikealocal.com/how-to-plan-a-trip-to-italy/

The Italian On Tour. (2023). *Flights to Italy: 5 things you need to know before booking*. Retrieved from https://www.theitalianontour.com/flights-to-italy-5-things-you-need-to-know-before-booking/

Italian Tours. (n.d.). *Need to know*. Retrieved from http://www.italiantours.us/NeedToKnow.html

Italy Explained. (n.d.). *Places to stay in Italy: What those accommodation terms mean.* Retrieved from https://italyexplained.com/places-to-stay-in-italy/

Italy Foodies (2023, February 19). *A foodie tour of Italy: 31 bucket list food experiences.* Retrieved from https://www.italyfoodies.com/blog/foodie-tour-of-italy-top-food-experiences

ITALY IRL (2022, July 19). *Ultimate guide to the cost of family vacation in Italy.* Retrieved from https://www.italyirl.com/ultimate-guide-to-the-cost-of-family-vacation-in-italy/

Journey of Doing. (n.d.). *Florence travel blog.* Retrieved from https://www.journeyofdoing.com/florence-travel-blog/

The Knot in Italy. (2019). *Blush 03.* Retrieved from https://www.theknotinitaly.it/wp-content/uploads/2019/03/blush-03.pdf

La Rosa Works. (n.d.). *Quotes about Sicily.* Retrieved from https://www.larosaworks.com/quotes-about-sicily.php

Lapham's Quarterly. (n.d.). *Writing in stone.* Retrieved from https://www.laphamsquarterly.org/arts-letters/writing-stone

Live the World. (n.d.). *Most wildly romantic Italian getaways.* Retrieved from https://www.livetheworld.com/post/most-wildly-romantic-italian-getaways

Look and Learn. (n.d.). *Veni, vidi, vici." (I came, I saw, I conquered): Julius Caesar's letter to the Roman Senate.* Retrieved from https://www.lookandlearn.com/history-images/A006798/-Veni-vidi-vici-I-came-I-saw-I-conquered-Julius-Caesars-letter-to-the-Roman-Senate

MAXXI - National Museum of 21st Century Arts. (2024). *Mission.* Retrieved from https://www.maxxi.art/en/mission/

M24o. (n.d.). *To do in Italy: Cinque Terre.* Retrieved from https://www.m24o.net/to-do-in-italy/cinque-terre/

Meer. (n.d.). *Michele De Lucchi.* Retrieved from https://www.meer.com/en/47567-michele-de-lucchi

Meer. (n.d.). *Miltos Manetas.* Retrieved from https://www.meer.com/en/38355-miltos-manetas

Meer. (2019). *Al norte de la tormenta.* Retrieved from https://www.meer.com/en/55417-al-norte-de-la-tormenta

Meghan the Traveling Teacher. (n.d.). *Tips for renting a car in Italy.* Retrieved from https://meghanthetravelingteacher.com/tips-for-renting-a-car-in-italy/

Michelin. (2024). *Michelin Guide Italy 2024.* Michelin Travel Partner.

Money.com. (n.d.). *Best travel insurance.* Retrieved from https://money.com/best-travel-insurance/

Mom in Italy. (n.d.). *Uber in Italy.* Retrieved from https://mominitaly.com/uber-in-italy/

Mom in Italy. (2024). *Best places to visit in Italy with kids – by a mom in Italy.* Retrieved from https://mominitaly.com/best-places-to-visit-in-italy-with-kids/

Mountains, D. (n.d.). *Lake Garda multisport adventure.* Retrieved from https://www.dolomitemountains.com/en/browse-experiences/lake-garda/lake-garda-multisport-adventure

Mumsnet. (n.d.). *To find it annoying when guests start eating before the host has finished serving*. Retrieved from https://www.mumsnet.com/Talk/am_i_being_unreasonable/2274733-to-find-it-annoying-when-guests-start-eating-before-the-host-has-finished-serving

Murphy, R. (Director). (2010). *Eat pray love* [Film]. Columbia Pictures.

My Cinque Terre. (n.d.). *Cinque Terre*. Retrieved from https://www.mycinqueterre.com/cinque-terre/index.html

Navager. (n.d.). *3 days in Venice*. Retrieved from https://www.navager.com/post/3-days-in-venice

Nelmondo, J. (2024, January 10). *The 6 most romantic things to do in Italy for couples*. WanderWisdom. Retrieved from https://wanderwisdom.com/travel-destinations/Things-to-Do-in-Italy-for-Couples

Nolan, E. H. (1864). The liberators of Italy: Or, the lives of General Garibaldi; Victor Emmanuel, King of Italy; Count Cavour; and Napoleon 3., Emperor of the French. In *Google Books*. J. Virtue.

Norwegian. (n.d.). *On-board seat reservation*. Retrieved from https://www.norwegian.com/en/travel-info/on-board/seat-reservation/

Oliver's Travels. (2019). *Must-know packing tips for family travel*. Retrieved from https://www.oliverstravels.com/blog/packing-tips-for-family-travel/

Order Sons and Daughters of Italy in America (n.d.). *Italian villages in Molise will pay you $27,000 to move there*. Retrieved from https://orderisda.org/culture/italian-living/italian-villages-in-molise-will-pay-you-27000-to-move-there/

Östenberg, I. (2013). VENI VIDI VICI AND CAESAR'S TRIUMPH*. *The Classical Quarterly*, *63*(2), 813–827. Retrieved from https://doi.org/10.1017/S0009838813000281

Pasolini, P. P. (Director). (1975). *Salò, or the 120 days of Sodom* [Film]. United Artists.

Pei, M. (1965). *The story of language*. Lippincott.

Perfetto Traveler. (n.d.). *Basilicata and Calabria by Perfetto*. Retrieved from https://www.perfettotraveler.com/travel-trade-hotels/basilicata-and-calabria-by-perfetto/

Podroze Po Europie. (n.d.). *Cinque Terre: Practical information*. Retrieved from https://www.podrozepoeuropie.pl/cinque-terre-informacje-praktyczne/

Prof. Hedgehog's Journal. (2017). *The last Medici*. Retrieved from https://professorhedgehogsjournal.uk/2017/02/07/the-last-medici/

Proihof. (n.d.). *Mountain bike holiday in the Dolomites: Discover the Funes Valley actively*. Retrieved from https://www.proihof.com/en/mountain-bike.html

Pubblico Italian Eatery. (n.d.). *Italian food and wine: A pairing guide*. Retrieved from https://www.pubblicoitalianeatery.com/blog/italian-food-and-wine-a-pairing-guide

Quora. (n.d.). *Do Italians use a fork and spoon to eat pasta?* Retrieved from https://www.quora.com/Do-Italians-use-a-fork-and-spoon-to-eat-pasta

Quora. (n.d.). *Is it inappropriate to cover the plate & silverware with your napkin after eating?* Retrieved from https://www.quora.com/Is-it-inappropriate-to-cover-the-plate-silverware-with-your-napkin-after-eating-My-logic-says-its-rude-to-subject-your-server-of-looking-at-the-dish-you-had-eaten-from

Quora. (n.d.). *What are some great parts of Sardinia that I should visit?* Retrieved from https://www.quora.com/What-are-some-great-parts-of-Sardinia-that-I-should-visit

Reflecteddetcelfer. (2009). *Volare - Domenico Modugno - Nel blu dipinto di blu.* [Video]. YouTube. https://www.youtube.com/watch?v=t4IjJav7xbg

Renzulli, M. (2024). *Searching for Italy: All the places Stanley Tucci went in season 1.* Italofile. Retrieved from https://www.italofile.com/searching-for-italy-stanley-tucci-season-1/

Rick Steves Community. (n.d.). *Carrying identification in Italy.* Retrieved from https://community.ricksteves.com/travel-forum/italy/carrying-identification-in-italy

Rick Steves Community. (n.d.). *Passports - check-in at hotel and can we leave them in room?* Retrieved from https://community.ricksteves.com/travel-forum/italy/passports-check-in-at-hotel-and-can-we-leave-them-in-room

Rick Steves Community. (n.d.). *Should I buy advance train tickets with all the strikes?* Retrieved from https://community.ricksteves.com/travel-forum/england/should-i-buy-advance-train-tickets-with-all-the-strikes

Rick Steves Community. (2017). *Need to carry passport all the time?* Retrieved from https://www.tripadvisor.com/ShowTopic-g187791-i22-k6630449-Need_to_carry_passport_all_the_time-Rome_Lazio.html

Road Reel. (n.d.). *Guide to visiting Procida Island, Italy.* Retrieved from https://www.theroadreel.com/guide-to-visiting-procida-island-italy/

Road Reel. (n.d.). *Is Calabria safe?* Retrieved from https://www.theroadreel.com/is-calabria-safe/

Road Reel. (n.d.). *Renting a car in Palermo: Driving tips.* Retrieved from https://www.theroadreel.com/renting-car-in-palermo-driving-tips/

Sander. (2021, November 10). *The essential solo travel packing list in 2023.* Ars Currendi. Retrieved from https://www.arscurrendi.com/solo-travel-packing-list-2023/

Savoring Italy. (n.d.). *Naples, Italy.* Retrieved from https://www.savoringitaly.com/naples-italy/

Savoring Italy. (n.d.). *Pisa, Italy.* Retrieved from https://www.savoringitaly.com/pisa-italy/

Savoring Italy. (n.d.). *San Fruttuoso travel guide.* Retrieved from https://www.savoringitaly.com/san-fruttuoso-travel-guide/

Savoring Italy. (n.d.). *Travel to Milan.* Retrieved from https://www.savoringitaly.com/travel-to-milan/

Shakespeare, W. (1997). *Romeo and Juliet.* Simon & Schuster. (Original work published 1597).

S Money (2023, July 31). *What you need to know about currency in Italy: A travel money guide.* Retrieved from https://www.smoney.com.au/blog/currency-in-italy/

Solo Female Travelers Club. (2021). *Solo female travel stats.* Retrieved from https://www.solofemaletravelers.club/solo-female-travel-stats-2021/

SOS Tech (n.d.). *5 ultimate tips for emergency preparedness for traveling.* Retrieved from https://sostech.ca/5-ultimate-tips-for-emergency-preparedness-for-traveling/

SOS Tech (n.d.). *1 person 72 hr basic emergency kit SQ6009.* Retrieved from https://sostech.ca/product/sos-1-person-72hr-basic-survival-kit-sq6009/

Statista (n.d.) *Italy: Catholic Church adherence.* (n.d.). Retrieved from https://www.statista.com/statistics/1236961/relation-to-the-church-in-italy/#:

Statista. (2024). *Crime in Italy - statistics & facts.* Statista Research Department. Retrieved from https://www.statista.com/topics/4051/crime-in-italy/#topicOverview

Stevenson, R. L. (1883). *Treasure island.* Cassell and Company, Ltd.

Suhru Wines. (n.d.). *History of a grape: Pinot Grigio.* Retrieved from https://www.suhruwines.com/blog/History-of-a-Grape--Pinot-Grigio

Taylor Travel Management Group (n.d.). *Your VIP travel agency.* Retrieved from https://Taylortravelmanagement.com/.

Tickets Rome. (n.d.). *Colosseum.* Retrieved from https://www.tickets-rome.com/colosseum/

Toripines Travels. (n.d.). *Florence to San Gimignano.* Retrieved from https://toripinestravels.com/florence-to-san-gimignano/

Toscana SLC. (n.d.). *Italian feast: All saints day and all souls day.* Retrieved from https://toscanaslc.com/blog/italian-feast-all-saints-day-and-all-souls-day/

TouristSecrets. (2019). *Top 10 Italian islands you must visit.* Retrieved from https://www.touristsecrets.com/destinations/top-10-italian-islands-you-must-visit/

Trail Hiker. (2015). *Cinque Terre: Monterosso al Mare to Vernazza.* Retrieved from https://trailhiker.wordpress.com/2015/08/28/cinque-terre-monterosso-al-mare-to-vernazza/

Trainline. (n.d.). *Advance train tickets.* Retrieved from https://www.thetrainline.com/trains/great-britain/ticket-types/advance-train-tickets

Trainline. (n.d.). *How far in advance can I book?* Retrieved from https://help.raileurope.com/article/40642-how-far-in-advance-can-i-book

Trainline. (n.d.). *James Bond: No Time to Die filming locations and how to visit by train.* Retrieved from https://www.thetrainline.com/en-us/via/europe/james-bond-no-time-to-die-filming-locations-and-how-to-visit-by-train

Trainline. (n.d.). *Map of trains in Italy.* Retrieved from https://www.thetrainline.com/trains/italy/map

Trainline. (n.d.). *Strikes in Italy.* Retrieved from https://www.walksofitaly.com/blog/travel-tips/strikes-in-italy

Trainline (n.d.) *Trains in Italy | Buy Italy train tickets.* Retrieved from https://www.thetrainline.com/trains/italy

Travel and Leisure. (2020, November 12). *10 places where Italians travel in Italy, according to a local.* Retrieved from https://www.travelandleisure.com/trip-ideas/places-in-italy-where-italians-vacation

Trentino. (n.d.). *MUSE – Science Museum of Trento.* Retrieved from https://www.trentino.com/en/highlights/museums-and-exhibitions/muse-science-museum-of-trento/

Trip Advisor. (2013). *Beware! Thieves rife in central car park Pisa.* Retrieved from https://www.tripadvisor.com/ShowTopic-g187899-i577-k13381151-o10-

BEWARE_Theieves_rife_in_central_car_park_Pisa_Do_NOT_Par-Pisa_Province_of_Pisa_Tuscany.html

Trip Advisor. (n.d.). *Cinque Terre: Italian Riviera.* Retrieved from https://www.tripadvi sor.com/Attractions-g187817-Activities-Cinque_Terre_Italian_Riviera_Liguria.html

Trip Advisor. (n.d.). *Driving from Catania to Palermo.* Retrieved from https://www.tripad visor.com.ph/ShowTopic-g187888-i735-k14341382-Driving_from_Catania_to_ Palermo-Catania_Province_of_Catania_Sicily.html

Trip Advisor. (n.d.). *Florence treasure hunts.* Retrieved from https://www.tripadvisor. com/Attraction_Review-g187895-d11946168-Reviews-Florence_Treasure_Hunts-Florence_Tuscany.html

Trip Advisor. (n.d.). *Spiaggia di Fegina – Monterosso al Mare: Cinque Terre.* Retrieved from https://www.tripadvisor.com/Attraction_Review-g187820-d5256943-Reviews-Spiaggia_di_Fegina-Monterosso_al_Mare_Cinque_Terre_Italian_Riviera_Liguria.html

TripUniq. (2024). *Love your trip.* Retrieved from https://tripuniq.com/en/rome/love-your-trip/

UK Government. (n.d.). *Foreign travel advice: Italy.* Retrieved from https://www.gov.uk/ foreign-travel-advice/italy

United States Conference of Catholic Bishops. (n.d.). *Sirach 41.* In *New American Bible, Revised Edition.* Retrieved from https://bible.usccb.org/bible/sirach/41

Untold Italy. (n.d.). *Venice tourist tax.* Retrieved from https://untolditaly.com/venice-tourist-tax/

Untold Italy. (2024). *101 Basic Italian phrases for travel you need to know for your trip to Italy.* Retrieved from https://untolditaly.com/basic-italian-phrases-for-travel/

USAToday. (n.d.). *Italy villages.* Retrieved from https://www.usatoday.com/story/travel/ destinations/2017/10/19/italy-villages/776657001/

Versailles Tourism. (n.d.). *Visit and explore Versailles: The royal town.* Retrieved from https://en.versailles-tourisme.com/visit-and-explore-versailles-the-royal-town/a-town-to-discover

Viator. (n.d.). *Baths of the Queen Giovanna: Sorrento attractions.* Retrieved from https:// www.viator.com/en-IN/Sorrento-attractions/Baths-of-the-Queen-Giovanna-Bagni-della-Regina-Giovanna/d947-a18643/2

Viator. (n.d.). *Emerald grotto: Grotta dello Smeraldo.* Retrieved from https://www.viator. com/Sorrento-attractions/Emerald-Grotto-Grotta-dello-Smeraldo/d947-a18904

Vibo Valentia Province. (n.d.). *Costa degli Dei.* Retrieved from https://iitalycalabria.com/ vibo-valentia-province/costa-degli-dei/

Visa Reservation (n.d.). *Flight itinerary and hotel bookings for any country - Visa Reservations.* Retrieved from https://visareservation.com

Visit Italy. (n.d.). *The 5 most LGBT destinations in Italy: What they are and why.* Retrieved from http://www.visititaly.eu/places-and-tours/the-5-most-lgbt-destinations-in-italy-what-they-are-and-why

Visititaly.eu. (n.d.). *Female solo travel in Italy: 10 perfect destinations for women traveling on their own.* Retrieved from https://www.visititaly.eu/places-and-tours/female-solo-travel-in-italy

Vistoperitalia.esteri.it (n.d.). *Visto per l'Italia.* Retrieved from https://vistoperitalia.esteri.it/home/en

Viva Venetia. (n.d.). *Venice mask painting: Join our creative workshops.* Retrieved from https://www.vivovenetia.com/venice-mask-painting/

VRBO. (n.d.). *10 secluded beaches in Italy.* Retrieved from https://www.vrbo.com/en-gb/holiday-homes/destination-type/beach/10-secluded-beaches-in-italy

Walks of Italy. (n.d.). *The complete guide to Italy's festivals and celebrations (UPDATED 2024).* Retrieved from https://www.walksofitaly.com/blog/things-to-do/italian-festivals-guide

Walks of Italy. (n.d.). *Italy labor day.* Retrieved from https://www.walksofitaly.com/blog/travel-tips/italy-labor-day

Walks of Italy. (n.d.). *Strikes in Italy.* Retrieved from https://www.walksofitaly.com/blog/travel-tips/strikes-in-italy

Wanted in Rome. (n.d.). *British drivers warned of Rome mirror scam.* Retrieved from https://www.wantedinrome.com/news/british-drivers-warned-of-rome-mirror-scam.html

Washington Post. (2006). *The week's best travel bargains around the globe by land, sea, and air.* Retrieved from https://www.washingtonpost.com/archive/lifestyle/travel/2006/04/23/the-weeks-best-travel-bargains-around-the-globe-by-land-sea-and-air/61919c44-4c92-4dc7-915b-65d617f80e87/

Washington Post. (2016). *Italy's overlooked heel has a wealth of food, wine, and unique architecture.* Retrieved from https://www.washingtonpost.com/lifestyle/travel/italys-overlooked-heel-has-a-wealth-of-food-wine-and-unique-architecture/2016/04/21/49dfa9b4-0289-11e6-b823-707c79ce3504_story.html

World Baggage Network. (n.d.). *Italy traveler information.* Retrieved from https://www.worldbaggagenetwork.com/kb/italy/3-italy-traveller-information/

World Travel Guide. (n.d.). *Italy.* Retrieved from https://www.worldtravelguide.net/guides/europe/italy/

World Trips. (n.d.). *Should I get travel insurance?* Retrieved from https://www.worldtrips.com/should-i-get-travel-insurance

XE.com Inc. (1995-2024). *XE currency converter.* Retrieved from https://www.xe.com/currencyconverter/convert/?Amount=59.63&From=USD&To=EUR

Zicasso. (n.d.). *10 best places to visit in Italy with family.* Retrieved from https://www.zicasso.com/a/italy/de/family/ms

IMAGE REFERENCES

All images were provided by unsplash.com.

Made in United States
Orlando, FL
20 December 2024

56175824R00124